Counseling
for Substance Abuse
and Addiction

RESOURCES FOR
CHRISTIAN COUNSELING

RESOURCES FOR CHRISTIAN COUNSELING

VOLUME TWELVE

Counseling for Substance Abuse and Addiction

STEPHEN VAN CLEAVE, M.D.
WALTER BYRD, M.D.
KATHY REVELL, R.N.

RESOURCES FOR
CHRISTIAN COUNSELING

——————— General Editor ———————

Gary R. Collins, Ph.D.

WORD PUBLISHING
Dallas·London·Vancouver·Melbourne

Unless otherwise identified, all Scripture quotations in this volume are from the Holy Bible, New International Version. Copyright © 1983 International Bible Society. Used by permission of Zondervan Bible Publishers.

Permission to quote from the following sources is gratefully acknowledged:
Dying for a Drink, by Anderson Spickard, M.D., and Barbara R. Thompson, © 1985. Published by Word Books.
Where Is God When It Hurts?, by Philip Yancey. © 1977 by the Zondervan Corporation.
"I Am an Alcoholic," adapted from the original letter by Joseph Kellerman.
"The Twelve Steps," published by Alcoholics Anonymous World Services, Inc.
"A Question of Control" © 1987 by Vivian Brooks

An effort has been made to locate sources and obtain permission where necessary for quotations used in this book. In the event of any omission, a modification and acknowledgment will gladly be incorporated in future editions.

Library of Congress Cataloging-in-Publication Data

Van Cleave, Stephen, 1948–
    Counseling for substance abuse and addiction / Stephen Van Cleave, Walter Byrd, Kathy Revell.
        p.   cm. — (Resources for Christian counseling ; v. 12)
    Bibliography: p.
    Includes index.
    ISBN 0–8499–0593–1
    1. Substance abuse—Patients—Pastoral counseling of.   2. Narcotic addicts—Pastoral counseling of.   I. Byrd, Walter, 1949–
II. Revell, Kathy, 1948–   .   III. Title.   IV. Series.
    [DNLM: 1. Counseling. 2. Substance Abuse. 3. Substance Dependence.   WM 270 V222c]
BV4460.3.V36   1987
362.2′9—dc19   87-26656
                                                                          CIP

Printed in the United States of America

6 7 8 9 9 AGF 9 8

CONTENTS

EDITOR'S PREFACE

RECENTLY AN OLD FRIEND was telling me about his work as a counselor. "I have come to the conclusion," he said, "that our whole society is addicted. It comes up repeatedly in my practice, and so often the people involved are regular church attenders."

My friend added that he sees men who are addicted to pornography, young people addicted to music, some who seem addicted to eating, others addicted to masturbation, and a great number whose addictions involve alcohol and drugs.

When I first assembled a list of possible topics for these Resources for Christian Counseling books, it was clear that we would need a strong volume on substance abuse. But who would write it? Most of the books in this series are written by people who have been invited to write, but the proposal for this manuscript came unsolicited from the authors themselves. At first, the team had planned to write a popular book for parents and church leaders, but they soon saw an even greater need for a book on how we can effectively counsel substance abusers. By combining their experiences, technical knowledge, and areas of expertise, they worked as a team to produce a first-rate, readable, practical volume that can be especially helpful for Christian counselors.

The authors of this book work every day with addicted people—especially those who are involved in what has been called "the drug-abuse epidemic." Dr. Van Cleave is medical director of TOUCH Drug Rehabilitation, a Christian drug-treatment center in San Antonio, Texas. Dr. Byrd is medical director of the Substance Abuse Unit at Garland Memorial Hospital in Dallas where Kathleen Revell, a registered nurse, directs the unit and oversees patient management. As a team, these three authors have over forty years of cumulative experience in the evaluation and treatment of substance abuse. All three are committed Christians.

A concise consideration of substance abuse fits well into the Resources for Christian Counseling series. Each of these books is intended to deal with some topic that is likely to come up in your counseling. Written by counseling experts, each of whom has a strong Christian commitment and practical counseling experience, these volumes are intended to be examples of accurate psychology and careful use of Scripture. Each is intended to have a clear evangelical perspective, careful documentation, a strong practical orientation, and freedom from the sweeping statements and undocumented rhetoric that sometimes characterize books in the counseling field. Our goal is to provide books that are clearly written, practical, up-to-date overviews of the issues faced by contemporary Christian counselors. All of the Resources for Christian Counseling books have similar bindings and together they will comprise a complete encyclopedia of Christian counseling.

There may have been a time when we thought substance abuse was limited mostly to people outside the church. If this was true in the past, it certainly is not true today. The authors show clearly that anyone—church members included—can become addicted, often as the result of innocent choices. Young people who have been raised in the church (and sometimes their parents) often see no danger in experimenting with the drugs and alcohol that for many become an addition. Highly praised media campaigns urge young people to "Just Say NO!" to drugs, but nobody is taught *how* to say no in the midst of peer pressure. Substance abuse has become so widespread that most of us know of at least one person or family who has been deeply affected. Professional rehabilitation programs abound, but church leaders and Christian counselors often are called in to pick up the pieces of broken, angry, confused, and guilt-ridden families. This book will help the counselor in the slow, often painful, but potentially rewarding task of helping substance abusers and their families.

One of my students attended a Christian high school where he was invited to experiment with drugs; he got hooked. His family prayed and pleaded. They were reluctant to discuss their son's problems with other parents at church—parents whose teenagers appeared to be drug-free and moving up the academic ladder. Eventually, my student entered a rehabilitation program that was both effective and so expensive that his parents went heavily into debt in an effort to pay the bills. Could tragedies like this have been prevented? Could the parents have found solace and understanding in their church if there had been greater understanding of the powerful effects of alcohol and other drugs? Would money and time have been saved if an effective treatment program had been found sooner? This book would suggest that the answers to all of these questions is yes.

If you counsel with substance abusers or their families, this book will be helpful. If you want to understand one of the major social problems of our times, this book will be enlightening. If you have never knowingly met a substance abuser, this book will help you understand a problem that sooner or later you probably will encounter in your counseling ministry. The team of Van Cleave, Byrd, and Revell has cut through a lot of the rhetoric and confusion about substance abuse and produced a volume that is informative, helpful, and ever mindful of the biblical teachings about addiction.

Gary R. Collins, Ph.D
Kildeer, Illinois

INTRODUCTION

IT HAS NOW BECOME A DAILY OCCURRENCE for the newspaper headlines to chronicle another chapter in our national tragedy of drug abuse. We read of massive drug seizures, tragic deaths, and increasing drug use among our young people. It seems that we as a nation are bent on destruction. Yet despite this tragedy, both national and personal, we seem to be using more drugs than ever. This, despite the overwhelming evidence that drug abuse is deadly. The real question is: If drugs are so bad why do people keep using them?

The answer is that *drug abuse is not just a drug problem.* It is really a *people problem!* Cocaine, opium (heroin), alcohol, and marijuana all have been cultivated and used for centuries. They are now such a severe problem, in part, because we live in an age that has lost its spiritual compass. Drugs are more and more being used to fill the place in human hearts that only God himself can fill.

Addiction develops from an unhealthy choice of using drugs

as a coping mechanism for dealing with the pain of living. As a society, we have come to believe that having any kind of pain is unacceptable. In reality, pain is a normal and necessary part of life. Pain motivates us to change, to grow, to stay out of trouble. How we learn to deal with pain is most important. The sin of drug addiction is the *loss* of what we have been created to be.

Is drug and alcohol abuse just a problem for the non-Christian world? Unfortunately not. Some experts in the field believe that the problem is just as great in the church as it is in society. However, it is frequently covered up and its existence is denied. There is a stigma to drug abuse that somehow makes it a "worse" sin, and the users are "worse" sinners. Many have said, "This couldn't happen to my family because we're Christians."

Joe is a student at a major university. He is the third of four children. His parents are Christian missionaries in a foreign country. Joe is addicted to both alcohol and cocaine.

As a teenager, Joe returned to the U.S. from the mission field to go to high school; he lived with his oldest sister and her husband. He was very angry at his father because their personalities were totally different and they could not get along at all. He felt unloved and unwanted. As a sophomore he started drinking alcohol and found that it made him feel great and that it also took away the anger. By the time he graduated from high school, he had become an alcoholic.

Shortly after he started college he discovered cocaine—it was love at first sight. In order to pay for his habit he became a drug courier, picking up the cocaine in a nearby city and bringing it back to the campus for the dealer to sell.

By the time he reached his junior year of college, life became unraveled. His grades fell, several acquaintances were arrested for drug dealing, and his girl friend told him that he had to choose between "me or the drugs." He sought treatment and is now drug-free. His relationships with both God and his family are on the mend.

Yes addiction can happen to anyone. In this book we will attempt to provide answers to the important questions about drugs and why people use them. These include: What is drug abuse? What are the main drugs of abuse and how do they affect users? Why do people get hooked on drugs? How can people get free from drugs? How can you help drug users and their families deal with their hurt and anger? How can one "drug-proof" a family?

This is a complex problem, and the answers and solutions are not easy. Instead, the answers—when they come—are long-awaited and difficult. No one can claim to have all of the answers. Each person's problem with addiction is as unique as is each snowflake. However, there are many basic facts which are common to all types of drug abuse. There are also fundamental principles for dealing with the drug user and his or her addiction which apply to all drugs, regardless of how they are abused. The problem is not hopeless. Despite the pain, suffering, and despair brought about by drug use, answers and solutions are available. They are not easy, however, for either the drug users themselves or for their family members. Those involved in the problem must be prepared for many tears and much struggling.

The final answer for our national problem of substance abuse lies in a change in our values as individuals, from self-centeredness to God-centeredness. The personal answer to the tragedy of drug abuse is in establishing and maintaining a personal and vital relationship with God—for what is impossible for man to accomplish is possible by God's power! We hope that this is what you and your counselees will gain from this book.

Note to the reader: Some of the terms used in this book may be technical and difficult to understand. Appendix 1 and 2, provided at the end of the book, help clarify many of the terms unique to the substance abuser's world. All of the patients' stories are based upon real cases; however, names and details have been altered to protect confidentiality.

Counseling
for Substance Abuse
and Addiction

RESOURCES FOR
CHRISTIAN COUNSELING

CHAPTER ONE

NOBODY STARTS OUT TO BE AN ADDICT

INNOCENT CHOICES CAN LEAD ANYONE
INTO ADDICTION

"I hate myself. I can't believe I did this to myself," said the note left by Paul Mayotte. He also wrote that he had loved cocaine, "that white lady of death," more than anything. Hampden County District Attorney Matthew J. Ryan released excerpts of the nine-page handwritten letter, saying Mayotte's note indicated he wanted to warn young people to stay away from drugs.

"You've got to get them while they are young. My mom and dad were so right when they said one bad habit leads to another. I can't understand why I'm not dead already. I tried enough with cocaine . . . my lungs are gone . . . my nose is shot . . . I'm on my last roundup." To his brother, Thomas, Mayotte wrote: "Tom, I hope you let some kids read this letter. I was a good kid once upon a time, long, long ago. . . . I want to say once again, I brought all this onto myself. I never carried a gun. I never beat anybody. I never liked violence. I don't dig it. I'm sorry. . . . Give this to whomever, I don't know." After writing this note, Mayotte shot himself to death in his pickup truck—the day he was due to appear in court, in Springfield, Massachusetts on charges of conspiring to distribute cocaine.[1]

This tragic story highlights the fact that no one starts out to be an addict. This young man didn't plan for it to happen. He didn't plan to destroy his life—but he had, and he was unable to face the consequences.

WHY DO PEOPLE GET INTO SUBSTANCE ABUSE?

Why do kids get hooked? Why do adults get hooked? This is the $64,000-question of drug abuse. There is no easy, single answer. There are as many theories as there are researchers in the field of substance abuse. Whatever the reason, substance abuse starts with the choice to try drugs, to use them. One thing is known for certain—if people don't try or experiment with drugs or alcohol, then they will not become addicted.

We do know that people are most vulnerable to experimentation with drugs between the ages of twelve and twenty. If they don't get into drugs then, they will be less likely to do so as adults. However, more and more people are trying drugs for the first time as adults, and subsequently getting hooked. None of us is immune to drug abuse. If the circumstances are right, anyone at any age can get hooked on drugs!

Elaine was in her mid-fifties when she developed severe arthritis. Her doctor gave her codeine to treat the pain that she was experiencing. Before long, she was taking the codeine every day.

She also discovered that the codeine helped ease the

pain of her troubled marriage. She used this as her coping mechanism, despite the fact that she was a devout Christian. After two years, she realized that she was addicted and sought help.

She entered a drug treatment program and was successfully withdrawn from the codeine. More importantly, she received counseling and learned how to trust God rather than codeine to help her deal with the pain of her difficult marriage.

Seven Factors that Lead to Drug Abuse

We have identified seven factors that have a major impact on both adolescents and adults and increase their chances of deciding to try drugs. These are:
1. The disordered family,
2. Lack of self-esteem,
3. Peer pressure,
4. Experimentation (curiosity),
5. Cultural influence,
6. Parental drug abuse,
7. Lack of moral and spiritual values.
Though most of these factors involve the family, this does not mean that parents are to blame for their child's (either teenage or adult) addiction.

None, some, or all of these factors may be operating within the life of the person who starts using drugs. These are *not causes* of drug abuse—the unfortunate choice to try drugs and then to continue using them is the main "cause." If the person's body/brain chemistry likes the drug, he or she is on the downhill road—the disease process of addiction overrides the ability to make choices. However, just because these factors are present in a person's life does not mean that he or she will become a drug user. Likewise, having a healthy home atmosphere will not guarantee a drug-free child (but it is the best antidote in our drug-infested society).

1. The disordered family.

Christine is a 14-year-old who has been using pot for the past two years, and is facing suspension from school for hitting another student. She told her counselor that she hit the other child out of anger about her home life. She is the second oldest of six children whose mother died while giving birth to her youngest brother. She lives with her father, an alcoholic who regularly beats her and her older sister.

On a wide scale, the American family unit is no longer intact. Half of all children are growing up in single-parent families, usually with a mother who must work and, therefore, is frequently absent. The extended family—aunts, uncles, grandparents, etc.—is no longer available as a support group, since the average family moves every five years. Perhaps no other nation has witnessed such destruction of the intact family as has ours.

The family is the center of the child's universe, and chaos in the family will spill over into the child's life. The family that is most likely to "produce" a drug-using child is one in which the father is absent (usually through divorce). The mother is left with all the burdens of both child rearing and working. This makes it very difficult for her to meet the emotional needs of her children.

Problems are also more likely when discipline is either excessively harsh or excessively lenient. If the family is not intact, there may be a lack of closeness, a lack of bonding between parent and child. Is it any wonder then that the child seeks an escape from the miseries of home? Many kids will escape into positive activities such as sports, academics, or work, but others seek to escape through drugs.

The family is equally important for the emotional health of adults, and they are not immune to the stresses caused by a disordered family. The traumas of divorce, the death of a spouse or a child, the effects of major illness, the isolation due to moving to a new location, or the children growing up and leaving home—all can be factors in an adult's becoming dependent upon drugs or alcohol to escape.

2. Lack of self-esteem. If the family is the center of the child's universe, which it is, then self-esteem is the center of the child's being. Self-esteem can be defined as how one feels about one's self. Children growing up in a troubled family

cannot feel good about themselves. They feel that there must be something wrong with them or they would not be in such a situation. They also feel a great sense of guilt and responsibility for their parents' problems.

Affluence is another great destroyer of self-esteem. When parents spend too much time in the pursuit and maintenance of their possessions and lifestyles, there is less time for relationships that are vital to the healthy emotional development of their children. Children probably need their parents' time and attention more than ever during the teen years. If parents give them money or things, but not themselves, they really have given them a message that says: "You're not as important as my job, social life, etc."

Adolescence is a time of assault on self-esteem. School, sports, acne, money (too much or too little), the opposite sex, hormones, friction with parents, all take their toll on the adolescent psyche. This is magnified by the fact that our culture bases a person's worth on his or her performance and not on the person. If people feel bad about themselves they often try drugs. While they are high, nothing can bother them, nothing can hurt them.

> Jerry was short and unattractive as a teenager. He felt inferior to other kids and subsequently got into drugs. He started with pot, but graduated to heroin before his twentieth birthday. He entered a drug treatment program, but failed to get drug-free. Sadly, he died of a heroin overdose at age twenty-three.

Adults need healthy self-esteem just as much as teens do. However, they frequently cover up the need. They also tend to derive it from areas outside the family, especially from career. In our success-oriented society, a major cause of adult loss of self-esteem is failure, such as at work, with a spouse, or as a parent. Drugs can help cover over the pain of failure.

3. Peer pressure. Drug abuse is like a disease in that it is spread from person to person. We have never had a patient who said to us, "I want to get hooked on drugs," or "I want to become an alcoholic." Initially, when people first start using a

drug or alcohol, someone else has to supply them with, and teach them how to use it. This is where peer pressure comes in—it is hard for a teenager to say no to friends who offer drugs. This happens despite good parental teaching, the right values, and even fear of using drugs. Adolescents just don't want to be "uncool," or appear to be square. They want to be accepted, and if their friends are into drugs and alcohol, it is very difficult to say no.

Rick was thirteen when he went to a nearby apartment, selling door-to-door to earn spending money. He was invited in by an 18-year-old acquaintance and asked if he wanted to get "loaded." Not wanting to appear naive, he smoked his first joint. He went on to use all of the drugs of abuse. Many years later he is finally drug free. However, along the way he failed at several marriages, lost numerous jobs, and brought himself and his family years of grief and heartache.

Adults don't want to be "uncool" either; that is why we all strive so hard to "keep up with the Joneses." We are just more sophisticated in how we exert peer pressure, and in how we respond to it. We also find it difficult to say no. When was the last time you bought something that you absolutely did not need from a pushy salesperson?

Linda didn't know that her husband-to-be was a heroin addict. She herself had never used drugs or alcohol. After she had been married several months, she learned of her husband's addiction. Several years later, she decided to try heroin herself and quickly became addicted.
She and her husband entered a treatment program and after a difficult year of outpatient detoxification, she became drug free. He did not. She attributed her freedom to her newfound faith in God and is now helping other addicts to become drug free.

4. Experimentation. Adolescence is a time of curiosity, a time to find out what the world is really all about. The wisdom

of all authority figures (parents, teachers, pastors, doctors—everyone) is highly suspect. Teenagers want to find out for themselves about drugs—are they really *that* bad? *If they are, why do all my friends do them?* they ask.

> George was twelve when he went to a friend's house. The friend's older brother was in the attic smoking pot, and invited the boys to try it. He did and found that he liked it, and spent the next ten years struggling with it, before becoming drug free.

Unfortunately, until recently, the media—such as movies, commercials, and music lyrics—made drug and alcohol use appear fun, harmless, and safe. The implied message was, "Why not try them and find out for yourself what they are all about?" Adding to this problem is the fact that the consequences of drug abuse are not always apparent at first, thus giving the appearance of safety.

5. Cultural influence. America is a drug-using society. It is estimated that 25 percent of television ads are for some kind of drug or medicine. The message is: "If you don't feel good, take this medication." And that is precisely what millions do every day. Many physicians are happy to oblige their patients with a dazzling array of sleeping pills, stimulants, tranquilizers, and pain pills. An estimated 5.2 million adults are now dependent upon these medications.[2] Unfortunately, their "pusher" is all too often their personal physician. It's easier to write a prescription than it is to take the time to find out what's going on in a patient's life and then offer nondrug alternatives.

This phenomenon is not new. Coca-Cola derived its name from cocaine which was included in the drink as a mild stimulant. It was advertised as "the ideal brain tonic." In 1906, caffeine replaced cocaine when cocaine became an illegal drug.

Think of how advertising is used to promote consumption of alcoholic beverages. Their use is always shown in association with attractive, friendly people in beautiful surroundings, thus implying that we will be that way if only we drink their booze. Most of us don't ever see the negative consequences—the twenty-five thousand who die every year on our highways because of drunk driving, or the violent crimes, such as spouse and child abuse.

Bubba Smith, a retired pro football star, announced in the summer of 1986 that he was giving up his lucrative advertising contract with a certain beer manufacturer.

Why? In 1985, he was the homecoming marshal at his college alma mater. When he was introduced at half-time, the students proceeded to shout the slogans from the beer commercials which he had previously recorded.

"I didn't know what it was doing to the kids," he said. "Once I saw it, I thought, I'm not going to do it anymore. How much money can you make before you ruin everybody?"[3]

6. Parental drug use. If your counselee had a parent who had problems with drugs or alcohol then he or she has a much higher likelihood of following in that parent's footsteps. Forty percent of substance abusers have grown up in such families. This has been observed even in those who were born to alcoholic parent(s) but were subsequently raised from infancy in nondrinking families. This also occurs among adult children of alcoholics who never had a problem with alcohol until they were well into adulthood. Adult children of alcoholics also develop other emotional problems (see chapters 6 and 8).

Ed grew up in an average middle-class family. His father was a heavy drinker, a "closet drinker," and most of his friends knew nothing about his alcoholism.

As an adult Ed rarely drank alcohol, and never got drunk. However, at age 45 he developed medical problems and also started drinking heavily. He progressed to full-blown alcoholism, destroying his marriage and estranging his children in the process.

The reasons behind this are not totally clear. Both parental example and influence, along with heredity, are operating to lead a person toward drug abuse. We do not know whether the environment or genes plays the greater role in this. This does not mean that getting into drug abuse is predetermined, but it does mean that if a family has a drug-using or alcoholic history, drugs and alcohol should be avoided at all costs and should not be kept around the house if possible, due to the high risks.

Bill was a 40-year-old heroin addict in a drug rehabilitation program. He tried to hide his addiction from his teenage son, so that the son would not follow in his footsteps. He even railed against drugs, hoping to convince the boy of the dangers. Unfortunately, the son also started using heroin by the age of 18.

7. Lack of moral and spiritual values. According to the late Francis Schaeffer, America is living in a post-Christian era. This, despite the fact that 80 percent of the adults in the U.S. polled by George Gallup claimed to be Christians. Jesus said, "where your treasure is, there will your heart be also." In the 1980s the "treasure" of most Americans is pleasure and wealth. Even the church is embracing this.

Man's significance comes from his relationship to his God and to his fellow man, not from the abundance of his possessions or pleasures. The Old Testament shows that Israel plunged pitifully when its rulers and its people ran after wealth. *The Rise and Fall of the Roman Empire* demonstrates the fact that when Rome's leaders only lived for carnal and material pleasure, the once-great empire was no match for the forces that would destroy it. The society that pursues affluence is ultimately destroyed by it. We in affluent, Western society are no different. Someone has captured the acquisitive character of modern-day, "civilized" America in the facetious motto: "He who dies with the most toys, wins." Our pursuit as a people after materialism proves that many have lost all spiritual perspective, and when that happens the slide into self-serving behavior including drug abuse comes easily.

Changes in our morals and values have poured gasoline on the fire of drug abuse. Many people involved in facilitating the availability of drugs (bankers, pilots, truck drivers, for example) do so because of the money. Then they rationalize their participation by saying: "If a person wants to use drugs, that is their own business." Without the "help" of all these people, drugs would be a lot harder to find—instead of being so readily available. According to Gene Anderson, of Seattle, Washington, a U.S. attorney who has prosecuted drug cases involving prominent businessmen in that city, each purchaser of drugs, (because of the vast amounts of money ultimately involved), plays some role in supporting the powerful criminal networks which supply drugs worldwide.[4]

Andy grew up in a middle-class family. He learned a trade, got married and started a family. He prospered financially and life went well—until a friend introduced him to cocaine. He decided to try it, and was soon hooked. After his addiction destroyed his marriage, his finances, and his career, he entered treatment. He began to read the Bible and pray for the first time in his life. He stated to his physician that he wished he had discovered God earlier in life, and thus might have spared himself and his family all of the misery of drug abuse.

THE STEPS TO DRUG ADDICTION

A person does not usually become addicted to drugs and alcohol overnight. (Note: Whenever the word *drugs* is used, the authors mean drugs *and* alcohol.) The process begins with the first use of the drug and insidiously continues through a series of steps. First, there's experimentation; then there's progression from occasional use to regular use. Finally, it results in full-blown dependence or addiction. (See Table 1.)

These steps vary in the time required to take them. They may require twenty years in an alcoholic who starts drinking as an adult. They can also move at light-speed in the person who tries crack, a form of cocaine. In one study of cocaine addicts, over half of those who tried crack and called the cocaine hotline said that they had "fallen in love" with the drug the very first time they had used it.[5] The reader is encouraged to study Appendix 7 where we have included a chart which details specifically the steps into addiction and recovery from alcoholism.

Adults and adolescents progress through the same steps. However, adolescents frequently move through the addiction process ten times faster than adults. Adolescents don't have the same internal controls that adults usually have. The adolescent brain and nervous system is still developing and is more susceptible to the effects of drugs. This is why a teenager can become an alcoholic or a "pot head" in just a few months.

Step 1: Experimentation

This is where it all begins. If people don't try drugs, they will never get hooked. Unfortunately, many do try drugs for the reasons we have already listed. Fortunately, many people find that they don't like the feeling that a drug produces, or they don't like being under its influence, and stop after the first few times.

But many accept the offer of the popular commercial: "Try it, you'll like it"—and they find that they do like the good feeling they get. This euphoria brings a person back for more; and continued use leads to the second step. The drugs most commonly used in this step are alcohol and pot, and at this stage they are used more often on the weekends than at any other time.

Step 2: Occasional Use

This step is sometimes called "social use." The drug user is still feeling his or her way along, frequently guided by more experienced peers, learning how to use the drug "properly" and how to enjoy the high. (Often in the beginning users will feel badly rather than euphoric, thus they must be coached on how to use the drug and what to expect.)

Use is still mostly with peers, now more frequent, but not daily. The user says, "I can take it or leave it," but is on the road to regular and uncontrolled use. Some people are able to remain at this level of drug use indefinitely, but little is known about them because they don't usually seek treatment. Many will eventually go on to the next step of regular use.

At this stage, other drugs are added or tried, including cocaine, speed, and the hallucinogens. This is called "polydrug use." With the exception of alcohol, few people use only one drug exclusively. Most use *many drugs,* depending upon the availability of the drug or the amount of money the user has to spend.

27

Persons may be fully addicted even though they do not use drugs every day. Such people lose control under the influence of their drugs and thus fulfill the definition of addiction (see Glossary). The severity of their illness is substantiated by the losses that result from their drug use. A case in point is the "weekend alcoholic." These people drink uncontrollably from Friday through Sunday but tell themselves and others, "I'm not an alcoholic because I only drink on the weekend." They may progress to daily use in time.

Step 3: Regular Use

Here, the use escalates to almost every day, if not daily. Drug users maintain their own supply of the drug and use it by themselves rather than only with friends or peers. The drug is now the major focus of their lives. However, when confronted by family or friends about the problem, they deny that any problem exists, or that it is as bad as it is.

All activities revolve around drugs and drug-using friends. The user is frequently intoxicated. Family relationships, school and job performance, health, and anything else of value are being destroyed. At this point, addiction is not far away, if not already present.

Step 4: Full-blown Addiction

Now the drug use becomes daily and usually all day. All of life revolves around getting, keeping, and using the drug. What has not yet been destroyed in step 3 soon will be. The abuser's brain chemistry has changed so that the drug is now a part of the "normal" functioning of the brain. If the drug is stopped, withdrawal sets in along with a severe craving for the drug. The user has to use the drug to "feel normal." He or she is truly hooked.

The four steps are a continual process. There's no virtue in saying, "I'm a social user, I'm okay. I won't get hooked." This is how John Gardner describes the process in his autobiography *Spin the Bottle: The Autobiography of an Alcoholic*:

The stuff which had given so much pleasure and power was now starting in on me; becoming not something to brighten the day, but a force as necessary as the air and the wind and the rain. However strong the will power, the liquor in the bottle was stronger, because by now my body needed it; shrieking for the daily ration as a drug addict's nerve ends scream for the needle. In junkie's parlance I was on main line.[6]

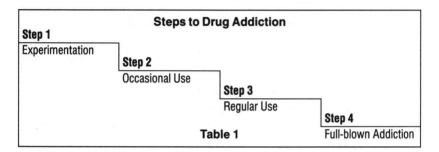

Table 1

Perhaps, worst of all is the fact that everything good in the drug abuser's life—family, friends, education, job, talents—is being destroyed. The road back is long and difficult, and many never make it back.

HOW DO DRUGS "TAKE OVER" A PERSON'S LIFE?

Why does a drug take over a person's life? Why don't the users recognize the danger that they are getting themselves into? The answer lies in the fact that we frequently operate on the basis of our feelings, and not just on rational thinking. This despite the fact that we like to consider ourselves rational, logical beings. This applies to all individuals regardless of social, educational, or occupational position. And this is where drugs get to us—in our feelings. (See chapter 4 for a more complete discussion.)

Since drugs make us feel so good, it is hard to say no once we have tasted of them. The feelings they bring are so good that we want to go back for more. Drug abuse has been called a "disease of our feelings." The drug abuser has learned to trust the euphoria, or the feeling of the drug experience.

Dr. Vernon Johnson of The Johnson Institute has beautifully shown how one's trust in the drug, and the feelings that it produces, develop. He describes four phases through which drug users progress on their way to full-blown addiction. Whereas the steps to addiction describe drug users' behavior, these phases describe their emotional state. They are: learning the mood swing, seeking the mood swing, harmful dependence, and using the drug to feel "normal."[7]

1. Learning the Mood Swing

This is the experimentation step, and here the drug user:

- learns that the drug can provide a temporary mood swing of euphoria
- learns that the drug will provide this euphoria every time
- learns to "trust" the drug and its effects
- learns to control euphoria by regulating the amount of the drug intake.

2. Seeking the Mood Swing

This is the occasional use step, and now the user:

- uses the drug at the "appropriate" times and places
- develops self-imposed rules about the use of the drug and adheres to them (for example, "I don't drink until after 5:00 P.M.")
- may suffer from physical pain (hangover) from overuse of the drug but is not yet feeling guilt
- can usually control the time, amount, and outcome of drug use.

3. Harmful Dependence

In this step of regular use, the drug user:

- experiences loss of control over his or her drug use and can no longer keep self-imposed rules
- violates his or her own value system, creating emotional pain and guilt
- loses insight into his or her behavior and uses rationalization to explain increasingly abnormal behavior

- develops increasing anger about himself or herself which results in growing emotional turmoil and projection of that anger toward others
- experiences increasing preoccupation with the use of the drug
- develops tolerance to the drug, which leads to ingenious ways of getting, using, and keeping the drug (sneaking drinks, hiding drug stash)
- undergoes deterioration of health, emotions, spiritual life, and family life.

4. Using the Drug to Feel "Normal"

During this final step, the drug user:

- has to use the drug to feel "normal," rather than just to get high
- has frequent loss of control and loss of memory due to drug binges
- finds that his or her tolerance for the drug increases even further
- experiences full-blown addiction
- frequently has paranoid-like thoughts, and behavior is totally unpredictable.

In this last phase substance abusers have reached the point where they feel that they are using the drug just to survive. The euphoric experience is either gone or happens infrequently, and the addiction process is now complete. *The users no longer have the drug; the drug has them.* This is the process of reaping and sowing, and is as certain as the law of gravity. At this point, drug users are powerless to stop using drugs without help.

Once a person is addicted, the drug becomes the center of life. Everything else takes second place to using and acquiring it. The drug now provides meaning and purpose. To quote Mary Ellen Pinkham, author of *How to Stop the One You Love from Drinking*, "Alcohol made me feel better about myself than any human being possibly ever could."[8] This is really a false sense of self-esteem caused by the drug. Deep down inside they usually feel totally worthless and frequently are filled with self-hatred.

WHAT IS THE "CAUSE" OF DRUG ADDICTION?

There is great debate over what drug abuse is. Many in the medical profession consider it to be strictly a disease. By that they mean that it has a cause (the drug), produces physical signs and symptoms, has a clinical course (what happens to the user), and brings harm to the health of the user. Without treatment, the "disease" is universally fatal; it is just a matter of time. The drug user can be treated for the disease by medical therapy and recover from the chemical addiction.

The difficulty with the medical-disease concept is that it seems to excuse the addict from any responsibility for the problem. After all, didn't the addict choose to try drugs? And after that initial use he or she had to make the choice to use it again and again, thus becoming addicted. If we were to look strictly at the drug user's behavior, we could conclude that the problem is really one of the wrong choices—a moral or spiritual problem. The solution then would be to start making the right choices and behaving the right way.

How can we reconcile the disease concept with the spiritual concept? The answer is that *drug addiction is both a medical disease (involving the mind and the body) and a spiritual crisis.* Therefore, the treatment of drug abuse requires both medical and spiritual therapy. You cannot treat one without the other. Sir William Osler, the father of modern medicine, put it best when he said: *"I treat, but God heals."*

Researchers in substance abuse have discovered very little agreement among theories as to the causes of addiction. Practitioners have even less agreement as to the course of proper treatment. "In spite of the variety of . . . perspectives offered to explain addictive behavior (e.g., moral turpitude, intrapsychic conflict, social deprivation, metabolic deficiency, developmental regression, pharmacological defense mechanisms), practitioners continue to apply their own ideas about addiction, addicts, treatment strategies, and the goals of treatment."[9]

As you can now see, drug addiction is a process then that

affects all aspects of a person's life—body, soul (mind), and spirit. First Thessalonians 5:23 identifies these aspects of man's nature. It affects the body through physical addiction, damage to health, and ultimately death. It affects the mind or soul through guilt, anxiety, fear, and depression. And it affects the spirit because when one is addicted to a drug he or she cannot have a close, vital relationship with God or with those who should be close, such as family members.

What should be our conclusion? Is there a simple cause of drug and alcohol addiction? The answer is no. The reasons that a person becomes addicted to drugs are complex and unique to each individual. Therefore, *the answer to the problem is not to lay blame, but to provide for a way out of the dilemma of addiction.*

There are, we must note, addictions other than drugs. These addictions, which are uncontrollable, compulsive behaviors, are just as damaging to the body, soul (mind), and spirit as are drugs. It is significant that our society tends to judge these forms of addiction less harshly than substance abuse.[10] These include:

overeating	workaholism
promiscuity	cultism
gambling	exercise
shopping	hobbies
churchianity (unhealthy religiosity)	

Some can hide their addiction more easily than the drug addict. Thus, they can appear more socially acceptable. If drugs are not your addiction, then what is?

The following prayer was given to the authors by a concerned parent in the hope that it would minister to those trapped in the snare of addiction, and also to those who desire to help them.

> Father God,
> We come before you today
>   in the name of all your confused children,
>   for whom alcohol and drugs
>   have become false gods.
> We ask that through your Love
>   they may gain release

33

and find their way
to wholesome living.
We bow our heads in humility,
mindful that each of us
knows the snare
of a destructive habit,
whether it be
food or tobacco or gossip,
gambling or grudge-holding,
ambition or greed.
Lord, let us see ourselves
not separate from those we call addicts,
but comrades in a common struggle,
bearing one another's burdens,
sharing faith and courage
on our imperfect journey
toward your perfect eternity.
Amen

CHAPTER TWO

WHAT YOU DON'T KNOW
COULD KILL YOU

HOW DRUGS AFFECT THE HUMAN BODY

In his mother's small, unkempt apartment off the major highway, the life of Manuel Saucedo is preserved only in a tiny portrait of Jesus with a funeral inscription on the back. "Oh gentlest heart, Jesus," a eulogy for the youth reads, "have mercy on the soul of thy departed. Be not severe in thy judgement." . . . Revelations that the young boy died August 17 of an allergic reaction to cocaine have stunned this agricultural community of about 16,000 and brought home the reality that drug problems are not confined to big cities. . . . "It's so shocking that it happened here in Hereford [Texas]," said Justice of the Peace Johnnie Turrentine. "And it's shocking that it happened to a 9-year-old."[1]

This tragic story reinforces the fact that with drug abuse there are no winners—only losers. Many end up with the ultimate loss—their lives. Why did this happen? Why will this scene be repeated many times in the future?

The drugs of abuse are very powerful chemicals that can have unpredictable effects on our bodies. They change the way a person feels, but they also kill, both unpredictably and unexpectedly. Once you put a drug into your body, you are at its mercy, playing a kind of chemical Russian roulette.

No one should be smug and think that "it can't happen to me." There is no standard of purity, no predictable potency for street drugs. And tragically, in the case of the innocent and curious younger brothers and sisters, these drugs aren't sold in child-proof containers.

WHAT ARE DRUGS?

Drugs are simply chemicals that can change something in the body's chemistry or internal makeup. We take "drugs" every day and never realize it. For example, vitamins, which are natural chemicals, are in our food and are absolutely necessary for the body to work properly. Without them we would eventually suffer severe or even fatal diseases. In this case these "drugs" are both necessary and beneficial.

We also use drugs that are prescribed by doctors to treat many illnesses, such as diabetes, infections, arthritis, or heart disease. This is a necessary and wonderful thing. Think of how your own life, or the life of someone close to you, has been saved by the "wonder drugs" of modern medicine. One major reason for the increasing life span in many countries is the widespread use of antibiotics which has saved many from an early death due to infection.

It is sadly ironic that one age group has recently shown a decrease in longevity—15- to 24-year-olds—and the principal cause is accidental death (auto, suicide, homicide, drug overdose). The common thread behind these statistics is the use of drugs, especially alcohol.

Drugs are harmful, or even fatal, if they are used for purposes for which they were not intended, or in the wrong way. This is what drug abuse is all about.

WHAT IS DRUG ABUSE?

Drug (or substance) abuse is the use of a mood-altering drug to change the way one feels. The drug may be inhaled, sniffed, swallowed, or injected. It may be legal or illegal, but it is not being used for legitimate or medical reasons.

If drugs are so powerful and so dangerous, why then do we have drug abuse? Why don't people stay away from them? The reason is that drugs change the way people feel. They do so in such an intense, pleasurable way that it is very difficult to say no, once individuals have started using them.

All drugs of abuse affect the brain. That is why they are called *psycho*active drugs, because they alter the feelings (mood-altering) and work primarily in an area of the brain called the *limbic system*. This is the part of the brain where the person's feelings originate. The drugs work by interfering with or substituting for the brain's natural chemicals, called *neurotransmitters*. These neurotransmitters are chemicals that carry a signal from one brain cell to another.

Whenever we experience "feeling good," it is because our brain cells have released a "dose" of a neurotransmitter. When that reaches its destination, at a *receptor* (another brain cell), we begin to feel good. This is both normal and natural and explains why we feel good after such things as accomplishing a difficult task or receiving affection from someone.

Psychoactive drugs cause their good feelings in several ways: by imitating the brain's neurotransmitters, by speeding up their release, or by prolonging their presence. This is what the process of getting "high" is all about. Once the drug is out of the brain, the effect is gone. However, when a person begins to use drugs regularly, the brain chemistry is altered by the drug and the drug becomes a part of the normal functioning of the brain. A vicious cycle starts—the more one uses a drug, the more the brain chemistry is affected by it, the more the person craves the drug, and the more he or she uses it. We know that the brain chemistry may not return to normal after a person quits using drugs.

> Bill was the vice-president of a corporation. He had been a heavy drinker for twenty years. By the time he was admitted for treatment he was showing signs of permanent brain damage, known as "organic brain syndrome." A CAT scan of his brain showed "cerebral atrophy," shrinkage of the brain as a result of alcohol abuse. When he returned to work his employer assigned him to sorting blue paper into blue boxes and red paper into red boxes. This was all that he was capable of doing.

Although this is an extreme example, many people will never be the same—they will have a permanent impairment in their ability to function in life. According to Dr. Forrest Tennant, they have what he calls Post Drug Impairment Syndrome, which he characterizes as a permanent chemical imbalance of the brain. "I see it primarily in persons who take drugs in their early teen years," he says, "but it can happen to anyone exposed to certain drugs for a long enough time." The syndrome is characterized by the inability to concentrate, maintain attention, hold a job, maintain personal relationships, achieve financial stability, handle stress, or remain in one location very long. It may also include fits of temper and antisocial behavior.[2]

> Jeff had been in the service almost four years, but his performance had severely deteriorated. When he had enlisted in the army, he did well in training and was on his way to becoming an excellent soldier. But after two years something began to go wrong. He developed a lack of motivation and of attention to detail, began to use his time inappropriately, and became ill-tempered with other soldiers.
> Jeff had been using marijuana heavily. The counselors treating him were very familiar with his condition; they referred to him as a "rubber head." He had "burned out"

his brain with drugs. He had the early signs of persistent brain damage from drug abuse.

WHAT IS DRUG ADDICTION (DEPENDENCE)?

Drug dependence is the compulsive desire to continually use a drug to either experience its effects (get high) or avoid painful realities despite adverse medical, financial, or legal consequences.

Drug addiction (also called chemical dependence) occurs when a person's brain chemistry must have the drug in order to function. If the drug user does not have the drug in his or her body, the neurotransmitter mechanism malfunctions. The person feels bad and is aware of an intense craving for the drug. If more of the drug is not taken, these symptoms intensify and physical withdrawal begins.

From a practical perspective, *addiction is a way of coping with painful reality that is self-destructive.* As we saw in chapter 1, the drug user does not start out with the intent to become addicted. Addiction develops from an unhealthy choice of drugs as a pleasure producer or coping mechanism. Alcohol, illegal or prescription drugs, and even over-the-counter drugs are initially taken to meet one's perceived needs or to deal with emotional or physical pain. The following anecdotes will show how this can happen.

George got up every morning at the age of fourteen to light the wood stove in the kitchen. His effort provided warmth for his parents and five brothers and sisters. One morning, the fire got away from him—George and one sister survived. At age fifteen, he began drinking and found that it helped relieve his guilt feelings. By age twenty-two, he was an alcoholic. Ten years passed before he entered a treatment program in which he learned how to deal with his sense of guilt, and withdrew from alcohol. He is still sober today.

Marie was a good skier and loved to sail down the slopes. One day she fell and injured her back, requiring surgery. Percodan (a narcotic) was prescribed for postoperative pain. Gradually, Marie increased her intake of pills and became addicted. In order to supply her habit, she carefully planned the refilling of prescriptions from four different physicians. One day she was found near death from an overdose. She entered treatment and is clean today after learning to manage her pain with biofeedback and nonnarcotic medications.

WHAT IS WITHDRAWAL?

Withdrawal is the unpleasant emotional and physical symptoms which occur when one is addicted and does not have enough drug in the system to satisfy his or her brain chemistry.

Withdrawal is what prompts the drug user to seek more drugs. He or she has to have the drug to feel "normal." Withdrawal symptoms are always unpleasant; depending upon which drug is being abused, they may include depression, fatigue, muscle aches, vomiting, insomnia, and irritability. We all have experienced these. However, they are more intense for the addict because of the changes in the brain chemistry. Thus the addict will do whatever is necessary to obtain more drugs to get rid of the symptoms. These symptoms do have one beneficial effect; they may drive the addict to seek treatment.

Clearly, drug use and abuse is very risky. Once a person starts using drugs, that person opens himself or herself to addiction. There is only one way to be sure of not getting hooked—never starting to use drugs in the first place.

In the following pages, we seek to provide answers with regard to the drugs of abuse. The counselor will perhaps want to refer to the chart at the end of this chapter while reading this information. The chart shows how the various drugs are to be classified and tells, at a glance, what are the medical and physical symptoms, the evidence of use, and the hazards of each class.

THE DRUGS OF ABUSE

The psychoactive drugs can be grouped into three categories based upon their major effect upon the brain. These groups are determined by their overall effect and not necessarily by the type of high they produce.

The first group is called *depressants* because they tend to depress one's mental functioning and awareness of the environment. Included are alcohol, sedatives, tranquilizers, sleeping pills, and narcotics. This grouping is arbitrary; other texts may group them differently.

The second group is *stimulants;* they stimulate mental processes and activities. There are two major drugs in this category: amphetamines and cocaine. Caffeine is a minor stimulant, and can also be addicting.

The third major group is called *psychedelics* or *hallucinogens;* they alter one's perception (awareness) of the environment. These drugs include: LSD, PCP, "Ecstasy," mescaline, and peyote.

Marijuana does not fit into any of the three groups. Sometimes it is listed with the psychedelics because it alters perceptions. However, it does not produce hallucinations.

Finally, two other types of drugs need to be included. Even though they are not usually considered major drugs of abuse, they are addicting and very harmful: *inhalants* and *nicotine.*

Alcohol

Alcohol is the generic term for the chemical *ethyl alcohol,* the psychoactive ingredient of all alcoholic beverages. Alcohol is found in three types of beverages: beer, which contains 3–6 percent ethyl alcohol; wine, which is 12 percent ethyl alcohol; and liquors (Scotch, bourbon, vodka, etc.), which contain 27–50 percent ethyl alcohol. Alcohol is also found in many over-the-counter medications, in concentrations as high as 25 percent.

In small doses, alcohol serves as a relaxant, and that is how many people use it. A small dose would be the equivalent of one twelve-ounce beer or a five-ounce glass of wine, or a one-and-a-half-ounce glass of liquor. This amount of alcohol does not usually produce any major change in behavior.

Medical scientists are still evaluating whether there are long-term benefits or side effects to this kind of alcohol use. However, a recently concluded study of eight thousand men who were observed for twelve years has shown some startling results. Those who drank less than fifteen ounces of alcohol per month (less than one drink per day) had twice as many strokes (brain hemorrhages) as those who did not drink at all. Those who drank at least thirty ounces of alcohol per month had three times as many strokes![3]

Alcohol, when consumed in excess, acts to depress the area of the brain that controls behavior. While under the influence the user experiences slurred speech, blurred vision, impaired muscle coordination, confusion, and impairment of memory. He or she talks excessively and is given to aggressive or hostile behavior. This effect varies: some people become "quiet" drunks, while others become belligerent and uncontrollable.

Alcohol intoxication interferes with the normal inhibitions that keep us from dangerous, harmful, or illegal activities. This is one reason that the majority of crimes and acts of violence are committed under its influence. Alcohol is not the cause, but being intoxicated makes those things easier by impairing one's self-control. It is converted by the body into secondary compounds called *metabolites,* which are similar to narcotics in their effect upon the brain. This may explain why alcohol is so addicting, despite the adverse consequences of continued, heavy use.

Alcohol is the most dangerous of any of the psychoactive drugs because it is a *toxin* (poison) that will damage most all of the body's muscles, the nervous system, the major organs (including the brain, liver, and heart), bone marrow, and the reproductive system. Heavy drinkers are more likely than nondrinkers to die from cancers of the mouth, throat, and digestive tract. In the United States alone, over six hundred people die *every day* either directly or indirectly from alcohol.[4]

Alcohol is very addicting—there are an estimated 12 million adult alcoholics and 4 million teenage alcoholics in the United States.[5] However, only 3 percent are skid-row "winos," which is the common stereotype. Although no cumulative figures are available, alcohol is also the most abused drug worldwide. Witness the crackdown on the sale and use of alcohol in the Soviet Union by its leader, Mikhail Gorbachev.

The alcoholic is more likely to be the responsible family man who drinks every night after work, or the housewife who drinks secretly at home. If you were to ask them if they are alcoholics they would reply, "Of course not. I can stop anytime I want to." But they never stop, and they have to drink more and more as time passes to satisfy their bodies' craving. (This is called *tolerance*: the brain's chemistry requires increasingly greater amounts of the drug to give the same effect.)

Sedatives and Hypnotics

This group of drugs also depresses brain function, which leads to a slowdown of thinking and activity. However, unlike alcohol, these drugs usually do not cause people to lose control of their behavior.

The drugs in this group include the barbiturates (Phenobarbital, Seconal, Amytal, etc.), the benzodiazepines (Valium, Librium, Dalmane, Tranxene, etc.), and the nonbarbiturate sedatives (Quaaludes, Placidyl, Doriden, Noctec, Equanil, etc.).

These drugs cause drowsiness, slurred speech, slowing of motor function and reaction time, and constricted pupils. They give a sense of calm, impair judgment and memory, and cause mood swings between passiveness and agitation. These effects last from a few hours to twenty-four hours, and overdose can cause coma and even death.

Their major medical uses include aiding sleep, reducing anxiety, and treatment of epilepsy. In the late 1970s, Valium and Librium were the two most widely prescribed drugs in the United States. These prescription drugs usually come from the family doctor. However, they are readily available on the street due to diversion from pharmacies, fraudulent prescriptions, and illegal manufacture. Many "pill addicts" go to several physicians in order to maintain their supplies. Some of these physicians are unwittingly manipulated while others unfortunately will give the patient whatever they ask for.

Even though these may be legitimate drugs, they can also be harmful. If they are taken chronically, these drugs will produce addiction and cause severe withdrawal symptoms. Withdrawal from barbiturates can be fatal if it is attempted abruptly once a person has become addicted. Additionally, when they are used in combination with alcohol, there is a high risk of overdose and subsequent death.

Narcotics

The narcotic drugs are used to suppress one's awareness of the environment, especially the awareness of pain. When used to treat severe pain, they are very useful and are usually not addicting. They can become addicting, however, when used for chronic treatment of pain. When used strictly for pleasure, they are rapidly addicting. The withdrawal symptoms are so severe with narcotics that once addicted a person will do anything to avoid withdrawal. To make the situation worse, tolerance quickly develops, which leads to addiction in a very short time, sometimes in only a matter of days or weeks.

Heroin (a morphine derivative) is the major drug in this category. Processed from the opium poppy, heroin is most often sold as a white powder which contains about 3 percent heroin; the rest of the mixture is usually made from milk sugar, starch, talcum powder, or whatever is available. Heroin is dissolved in water and then injected intravenously. In some parts of the world heroin is smoked, which has given rise to the term, "opium den."

Heroin causes almost immediate euphoria and a feeling of "I don't care." The pupils become pinpoint, speech is slurred, and the user becomes sleepy and frequently will "nod off" while sitting up. Chronic use causes suppression of appetite with significant weight loss—this despite an incessant craving for sweets. Heroin can cause sudden death due to interference with the breathing mechanism.

A new form of heroin is called "black tar" because it is a black, sticky mixture. It is also much more potent than regular heroin and is felt to be the major cause of the recent increase in deaths from heroin overdose.

While heroin is the most prominent narcotic, it is not alone; many prescription narcotics are also abused. Percodan, Darvon, Talwin, and Dilaudid are the favorites of those who prefer pills. Morphine, Demerol, and Fentanyl are the choices of the intravenous users, which includes many health-care professionals. All of these drugs, whether used orally or intravenously, are addicting and can cause sudden death when taken as an overdose or with other drugs.

Cocaine and Amphetamines (Stimulants)

The stimulants are drugs which "speed up" the brain and increase alertness, activity, and excitement. In doing so they cause a very intense euphoria. The major drugs are amphetamines (Speed) and cocaine (Coke). Amphetamines are synthetically produced drugs which have very limited medical use. In the past they have been used as appetite suppressants, but are currently only prescribed to treat hyperactivity and learning disorders in children. Cocaine is an extract from the leaves of the coca plant. Its medical use is that of a local anesthetic. The effects of both drugs include dilated pupils, profuse sweating, dry mouth, loss of appetite, indifference to pain and fatigue, and insomnia. They give the user the feeling that "I can do anything." However, when the high is over, he or she is left with a severe sense of depression called a "crash."

Coke and Speed are most commonly used in powder form and are mixtures of the drug and a diluting agent such as milk sugar. Cocaine is usually sniffed or "snorted" through a small straw or a rolled-up dollar bill. Cocaine may also be injected intravenously for an even more intense and quicker effect. Taken this way the effects are immediate and intense. The amphetamines are usually injected intravenously; however, they may also be snorted. Methedrine and Desoxyn are the most common amphetamines used intravenously. They are both referred to as "meth," "crystal," or "crank."

Amphetamines also come in capsule form (Benzadrine, Dexedrine, and Biphetamine) and may be taken orally; they usually do not cause the same intense euphoria as does speed in other forms. These drugs are frequently obtained from a physician for the purpose of weight loss. They are the only drug which is abused by more women than men.[6]

A cocaine high lasts from fifteen minutes to several hours, while an amphetamine high lasts four to twelve hours. The drugs may be used continually for hours or even days, nonstop, in what is called a "run." After the run, severe fatigue, depression, and paranoia usually occur. Some users will mix heroin with cocaine to try to lessen these effects; this is called "speedballing." Both of these drugs are very unpredictable and dangerous. Strokes, seizures, and sudden death from cardiac arrest are major complications of their use.

Cocaine may also be inhaled as a vapor using two different methods: free-basing or smoking crack. Free-basing is the mixing of cocaine with ether, boiling the mixture, and then inhaling the pure cocaine fumes, producing an instantaneous high. This is also very dangerous as the mixture can easily explode. Crack is a mixture of cocaine and baking soda which comes in pebble-sized rocks. It is then smoked, in either a pipe or a cigarette, releasing cocaine fumes, and causing instant and intense euphoria. Both of these forms of cocaine use are highly and quickly addicting.

Both amphetamines and cocaine are addictive and have a withdrawal syndrome. Unfortunately, in the recent past the belief was widespread that cocaine was not addicting. This belief was prevalent despite the fact that the first medical use of cocaine by Sigmund Freud was to treat morphine addiction, which resulted in one of the first documented cases of cocaine addiction.[7]

Last, but not least, of the stimulants is caffeine. Caffeine is found in coffee, tea, soft drinks, and chocolate, and is, worldwide, the most commonly used mood-altering drug. After oil, coffee is the world's second most valuable traded commodity.

Caffeine has two major effects on the body. The first is a release of adrenaline. This is the "fight or flight" hormone, which causes us to be more alert, have more energy, and feel stronger physically. Secondly, caffeine triggers the release of the neurotransmitter *norepinephrine*, causing mental stimulation. Interestingly, this is very similar to the way in which cocaine works.

We may become addicted to caffeine if we drink more than five cups of coffee, or its equivalent, per day. This represents an intake of approximately five hundred milligrams of caffeine. Caffeine withdrawal symptoms usually occur in the morning and include lethargy, grouchiness, headache, and sleepiness.[8] The symptoms are dramatically relieved by drinking a cup of coffee, a cola beverage, or whatever one's favorite source of caffeine might be.

Is coffee (caffeine) safe to use? Yes, as long as one limits the intake of coffee or its equivalent to less than five cups per day. Recent medical research has found a relationship between excessive coffee intake and heart attacks, as well as fibrocystic breast disease in women.

Marijuana (Pot)

Marijuana is a tobacco-like mixture made from the leaves of the plant *Cannabis sativa*. These leaves are crushed and rolled into a cigarette called a "joint" to be smoked. Marijuana is not a pure drug but rather a collection of similar chemicals called *cannabinoids* that are released when the marijuana is burned. There are over sixty different psychoactive chemicals in marijuana smoke, the most active of which is called THC (delta-9 tetra-hydrocannabinol or delta-9 THC). Hashish (hash) is the oil extracted from the leaves and contains a higher concentration of delta-9 THC. It is usually smoked in a pipe.

The marijuana high lasts two to four hours and produces a distortion of one's sense of timing, impairment of most motor skills and powers of reasoning, as well as confusion and forgetfulness. Additionally, the eyes are bloodshot, the pupils are frequently dilated, and appetite and thirst increase.

The euphoria gives the user the sense that everything is fine and that there are no problems. However, when the high is gone, the user is less likely to want to solve problems or achieve goals. Chronic use frequently results in paranoid thinking and behavior. Chronic users also have frequent respiratory infections and run the risk of damage to the reproductive organs.

The metabolites of marijuana stay in the body for several weeks and may still have an effect on brain functioning even though the high is gone. This is compounded by the fact that the potency (strength) of pot has increased from 1 percent THC 20 years ago to as high as 15 percent THC today, thus intensifying and perhaps prolonging the intoxication.

Pot is not the benign drug many think it is. It is addicting and produces a withdrawal syndrome, leaving users with a continual craving for the drug, despite abstinence. This may last for weeks after smoking the last joint. Pot also produces what is called the "amotivational syndrome"; users have no

47

goals or ambitions, a condition that frequently persists long after they have stopped using the drug. Some teenagers who have been heavy pot users, and who have died accidentally from other causes, have been found to have atrophy (shrinkage) of the brain at autopsy.

Hallucinogens (Psychedelics)

The hallucinogens alter the mind's perception of reality; they can cause one to see, smell, or hear things that are really not there. Although they have been used in psychiatric research, there is no accepted medical use for these drugs. They include: LSD (Lysergic Acid Diethylamide), PCP (Phencycledine), "Ecstasy" (MDMA, an amphetamine derivative), psilocybin, and mescaline. LSD, PCP, and Ecstasy are manmade drugs, while the others are extracted from plants or certain mushroom species.

The hallucinogens are usually taken orally; however, PCP can also be smoked (usually with marijuana). It is so potent that extremely small doses are all that one needs to get high. LSD is the most popular and most widely used of the psychedelic drugs. PCP use is increasing, despite its tendency to cause violent and uncontrollable behavior. Ecstasy use is also increasing, because of its reported aphrodisiac qualities.

Each of these drugs produces a distinct and dangerous high. LSD causes the user to take a "trip" during which all of the senses are heightened and time tends to stand still. Music can be "seen" and colors can be "heard." An LSD trip can also uncover deeply repressed fears, anxieties, and memories and can last from two to eighteen hours. These trips can be enjoyable, but they frequently cause severe panic and even psychotic thinking, which can lead to unpredictable behavior in which the users may accidentally injure or kill themselves because they do not know what they are doing. These bad experiences can recur after the intoxication has worn off, the so-called "flashback." Mescaline and psilocybin produce similar effects but are less potent and more difficult to use because they have to be extracted from a plant.

PCP, though it behaves like a hallucinogen, is a complex

drug that was developed as an animal tranquilizer and anesthetic. In humans it alters the perceptions of the outside world
so that the user feels that he or she is looking at things through
a backward telescope. The user is restless, agitated, and can
alternate between stimulation, mental depression, and hallucinations. While under the influence, the PCP user may be violent and exhibit super-human strength. After the trip, which
can last from two to fourteen hours, the user usually experiences amnesia concerning what happened. Death among users
is common, due either to accidents or suicide while under the
influence.

Ecstasy is the new kid on the block. First used as a psychiatric drug (research only) to enhance intimacy, reduce inhibitions, and improve self-esteem, it has now been removed from
clinical use because of its side-effects. These include insomnia,
fatigue, hypertension, confusion, paranoia, hallucinations, and
psychotic reactions. This has not prevented its use from increasing, especially among young adults.

Inhalants

Inhalants are chemicals that are inhaled as fumes in order
to produce their effect. The most commonly used inhalants
are the nitrates and solvents. Nitrates are legal and are sold
over the counter. Their main effect is to make the user feel
lightheaded, which usually lasts less than an hour. Nitrates are
very similar to the medical drug nitroglycerin. Nitrates are
most popular among high-school and college-age persons.

We do not yet know whether the inhalants are addicting, but
they do not seem to be a major problem. However, this is also
what was said about cocaine just a few years ago.

The solvents are much more dangerous. They include glues,
paints (especially spray paint), gasoline, cleaning fluid, and
any other volatile chemical that can affect the brain. Inhaling
solvents may cause sudden death, violent behavior, and permanent brain damage. They are most commonly used by grade-
school children and teenagers, even though in many areas their
sale is restricted only to adults. Certainly their use is not to be
ignored, considering their wide availability.

49

QUICK REFERENCE CHART ON DRUG EFFECTS

	ALCOHOL	MARIJUANA	COCAINE	HALLUCINOGENS
TYPES (OR NAMES OF THE DRUG)	liquor wine beer	grass weed hash joint pot	crack snow coke base	acid LSD PCP ecstasy peyote
MEDICAL AND PHYSICAL SYMPTOMS	• decreased inhibitions • impaired coordination • slurred speech • unsteady balance • stumbling walk	• euphoria (laughing) • hunger • dry mouth • red eyes • diminished concentration • impaired coordination	• increased heart rate and blood pressure • intense uplift of mood, followed by depression • restlessness	• confusion • disorientation • hallucinations (dreaming while awake) • panic • extreme agitation • nausea
EVIDENCE OF USE	• hangover • smell of alcohol • intoxication • erratic behavior	• cigarette papers • pipes • odor of burning incense or hemp rope • dried plant material	• white powder • glass pipes • razor blades • syringes	• capsules, pills • dusters (marijuana cigarettes with PCP sprinkled on top) • blotter squares
HAZARDS	• accidents • impaired judgment • medical injury (esp. liver) • seizures on withdrawal	• addiction • panic or paranoid reactions • possible reduction of motivation • effects on reproductive system	• cardiac arrest • stroke • seizures • paranoia • depression on withdrawal	• violent injury to self or others • emotional instability • flashbacks

QUICK REFERENCE CHART ON
DRUG EFFECTS (Continued)

NARCOTICS	AMPHETAMINES	INHALANTS	SEDATIVES
dope heroin horse junk morphine Dilaudid Demerol codeine	crank speed crystal uppers	glue solvents aerosols (paint) gasoline White Out nitrites	barbiturates tranquilizers sleeping pills downers ludes Seconal Valium

• drowsiness
• euphoria
• lethargy
• *In withdrawal*
  vomiting
  runny nose
  and eyes
  ''goose flesh''
	• racing thoughts
	• extreme
	  alertness
	• talkativeness
	• loss of appetite
	• increased blood
	  pressure and
	  heart rate
		• dizziness,
		  headache,
		  nausea
		• lack of
		  coordination
		• euphoria
		• confusion
			• sedation
			• decreased
			  heart rate
			• drowsiness
			• impaired
			  breathing
			• loss of
			  coordination

• syringes/spoons
  needle marks
• tourniquet
• illegitimate
  prescription
  bottles
• criminal conduct
  to procure money
  for supply
	• pills and capsules
	• loss of sleep
	• disrupted
	  appetite
	• agitation and
	  hyperactivity
	• irritability
		• loss of
		  concentration
		• poor muscle
		  control
		• odor of solvents
		  or sprays
			• excessive
			  drowsiness
			• pills and
			  prescription
			  drugs
			• slurred speech
			• confusion
			• anxiety
			  between use

• addiction
• death by
  overdose
• hepatitis or AIDS
  by needle
  contamination
	• addiction
	• extreme activity
	  followed by
	  fatigue
	• depression after
	  chronic use
	• paranoia and
	  confusion
		• suffocation
		• brain injury
		• nausea and
		  vomiting
		• unconsciousness
			• addiction
			• overdose can
			  be lethal, esp.
			  in combination
			  with alcohol
			• seizures and
			  death on
			  withdrawal

Nicotine

Nicotine, the active ingredient of tobacco smoke, is the most overlooked addicting drug. In fact, it is now considered to be as addicting as heroin. In the United States, 27 percent of the adult population regularly smokes cigarettes.

Nicotine acts as a stimulant to the brain, and this is apparently why addiction develops. Nicotine also affects the muscles, working as a muscle relaxant, which may explain why a smoker who feels uptight can relax by lighting up. The nicotine effect (high) lasts less than one hour, which also explains why the smoker must keep smoking, every twenty to thirty minutes. Interestingly, a smoker can sleep all night without getting up to smoke because the metabolites of nicotine stay in the body for about eight hours and prevent active withdrawal symptoms.

Nicotine withdrawal causes anxiety, headache, nausea, insomnia, irritability, lightheadedness, inability to concentrate, and an intense craving for cigarettes. These symptoms last from a few weeks to a few months, even years in some cases. Withdrawal may be worse for women than for men and is felt to be as difficult (psychologically) as is withdrawal from heroin addiction. Despite the tremendous efforts made by many to stop smoking, only about 25 percent of those who quit are able to stay off for at least a year.

While nicotine itself is dangerous, tobacco smoke is itself even more harmful. Cigarette smoking is a major cause of death and disability, especially those that are attributed to pulmonary and cardiovascular diseases. *Almost one thousand people die each day, directly or indirectly, from the effects of tobacco smoke.*[9] Unfortunately, cigarette smoking somehow opens the door to the use of other addicting drugs—most people who become addicted to the other drugs started first with tobacco as teenagers. The converse is also true—those who don't smoke usually don't become drug addicts.

The discussion of nicotine is not complete without a word about a new adolescent craze—chewing tobacco and dipping snuff. This may seem preferable to smoking; however, the effects of this form of tobacco on a person's mouth may be worse than that of cigarette smoke. Cancer of the mouth was previously seen only in older adults who used both alcohol and tobacco heavily. Now it is being seen in teenagers who chew tobacco. They may be even more susceptible to this deadly disease than adults.

Teens and adults need to be made aware that chewing tobacco can be just as harmful, if not more so, than smoking cigarettes. Baseball great Babe Ruth died of cancer at age fifty-four and some researchers believe that his death was caused by his use of snuff.

CHAPTER THREE

THE EQUAL OPPORTUNITY DESTROYER

THE MAGNITUDE OF THE DRUG-ABUSE EPIDEMIC

The inhabitants of the earth spend more money on illegal drugs than they spend on food—more than they spend on housing, clothes, education, medical care, or on any other product or service. The international narcotics industry is the *largest* growth industry in the world. Its annual revenues exceed *half a trillion* dollars—three times the value of all United States currency in circulation, more than the gross national product of all but a half dozen of the major industrialized nations! To imagine the immensity of such wealth consider this: A million dollars in gold would weigh as much as a large man. A half-trillion dollars would weigh more than the entire population of Washington, D.C.[1]

The above information is from the recently published book, *The Underground Empire,* by James Mills. Mr. Mills spent five years following and observing federal agents as they labored to reduce the flow of illegal drugs into the United States. He goes on to state, "Narcotics industry profits, secretly stockpiled in countries competing for the business, draw interest exceeding $3 million per hour."[2]

A person would have to be living on a desert island not to be aware of the problem of drug abuse. However, until the death of college basketball star Len Bias, in the summer of 1986, it seems that the majority of Americans did not believe that a real problem existed. Or if it did, it was somewhere else. Now we have finally decided to declare "war" on drugs, even if we are about twenty years late.

To quote a law enforcement officer in rural Oklahoma: "The only difference in the drug problem between bigger and smaller towns is that the denial is greater here. Unless it affects them personally, they don't want to know about it."[3]

It was the rebellion of the sixties that led to the widespread introduction of drugs into the youth culture. Somehow, we hoped that these drugs were harmless, just a passing stage of development. The wasted lives, ruined careers, unplanned pregnancies, the overdoses and accidental deaths (under the influence) have littered the landscape just like the great plagues of medieval Europe. It seems that Americans won't recognize a problem until they are nearly destroyed by it.

The destructiveness of drug use has been graphically detailed by researcher Denise Kandel of Columbia University. Since 1971 she has been following a group of sixteen hundred men and women who graduated that year from a high school in New York state. Some have never used drugs, some are occasional users, and the others are daily drug users. She found that by 1980 those who used marijuana daily were:

- More than twice as likely to lose or change jobs.
- More than five times as likely to have had at least one abortion.
- Two to three times more likely to have consulted a mental-health professional, and seven to eight times more likely to have been hospitalized for a psychiatric disorder.
- Arrested five times more for infractions other than driving violations, and their delinquency rate was seven times higher.
- Four times more likely to have dropped out of high school.
- More than five times as likely to be separated or divorced.

Commenting on her research, Ms. Kandel said, "The consequences of drug use affect every aspect of young people's lives."[4]

Drug abuse affects all of us, whether or not we want to admit it. To quote Mills again: "Enormously powerful criminal organizations are controlling many countries, and to a certain degree controlling the world, and controlling our lives."[5] This has been graphically and tragically illustrated in Colombia, where the drug-lords openly kill both national and local officials who oppose drug trafficking. In some Third World countries, drugs such as marijuana, heroin, and cocaine are their major export. In the summer of 1986, the government of Bolivia had to ask the U.S. government for an emergency loan, after it had conducted a major campaign against drug growers. It had lost its major source of foreign currency, and was unable to purchase necessary imports such as oil, food, and machinery.

In the United States, illegal drug sales exceed $100 billion, making it larger than any Fortune 500 corporation. Seventy-five percent of all crime is directly related to either drug use, drug selling, or related criminal activity. Many who will read this book have been victimized by an addict stealing to support his or her habit.

Most people know someone who has a drug or alcohol problem. Forty percent of families have a member who is using illegal drugs or prescription drugs, or who has a problem with alcohol. Half of all traffic accidents that result in either injury or death are caused by a driver under the influence of drugs or alcohol (sometimes both!). Approximately 250,000 people die each year, directly or indirectly, due to the effects of alcohol on their lives—second only to deaths due to heart disease.

Drug abuse knows no class, or economic or political boundaries—the deaths of John Belushi and David Kennedy tragically attest to this. The drugs of abuse are more readily available because of the involvement of so-called "straight" people in the drug culture.

> Drug Enforcement Administration investigators monitoring phone calls to the home of one of Seattle's suspected major drug dealers tapped into a conversation they never expected to hear. Orders from street sellers were one thing, but here was Thomas G. Allison, a prominent attorney, casually phoning in for what the investigators believed to be a quantity of cocaine. To their amazement, other eminent citizens were also weighing in with relatively small orders, their voices fearless.[6]

Drugs of abuse, including alcohol, are available worldwide. The October 6, 1986 issue of *Newsweek* detailed the growing problem in the Soviet Union of both alcoholism and heroin addiction. In the past these problems were denied as being nonexistent there. Drug abuse is growing overseas, in both Europe and the Third World countries. Sir Jack Stewart-Clark, a British member of the European Parliament, stated in a 1986 interview that there are between 1.5 and 2 million heroin addicts in Europe.

In Canada, illegal drug use is not as high as that seen in the United States. However, all the drugs of abuse are readily available. According to the Royal Canadian Mounted Police, outlaw motorcycle gangs are major sources of drug trafficking.[7] Alcohol is still the major drug of abuse, despite increased use of cocaine, pot, and psychedelics. Alcoholism is a major problem in remote areas, especially among native Indians.

Drugs are just as easily found in the rural United States as they are in the urban areas. The California attorney general's office released a survey in April 1986 which found a higher use of drugs and alcohol among rural high school students than among their urban counterparts.[8]

Drug abuse is not a new phenomenon; it has been around as long as man. The Sumerians made references to a "joy plant" in their early writings dating to 5000 B.C. This "joy plant" is believed to be the opium poppy, from which we get the legal drug morphine and its illegal cousin heroin. The Chinese first reported the use of cannabis (marijuana) in 2737 B.C. The Incas discovered the leaves of the coca (cocaine) plant by at least 1000 B.C., and chewed them for their effect as a stimulant (similar to our use of caffeine today). Although no date is available for the first use of alcohol, the Bible first mentions drunkenness in the story of Noah (Genesis 4), and the Code of Hammurabi, dating to 1700 B.C., lists laws against drunkenness.[9]

What is the extent of drug abuse in the United States today? Sixty percent of the adult population uses alcohol, and in that group there are 12 million alcoholics. In the teenage group, 5 percent of high school seniors use alcohol *daily* and there are an estimated 4 million teenage alcoholics! Most of these people are not skid-row tramps. However, they are alcoholics because they cannot control their drinking—it controls them.

When it comes to pot, around 60 million people in the United States have tried it and 18 to 25 million use it regularly. Because marijuana stays in a person's bloodstream for several weeks, it may well have an effect on a person's mental functioning even if he or she is not high at the moment.

At least 25 million people have tried cocaine, and 6 million are regular users.[10] The new form of cocaine, crack, is even more addicting and this number is sure to rise. This trend is already underway in the Bahamas where crack use led to a five hundredfold increase in the number of persons seeking drug abuse treatment between 1982 and 1984.

And let's not forget heroin. Even though cocaine is the glamour drug of our time, heroin is still around, with between a half million to a million users in the U.S. Amphetamines (speed), tranquilizers, and sleeping pills also have several million devotees. Prescription drugs, including the above, and narcotic pain medications are also abused by several million people. Last, but not least, are drugs like PCP, LSD, and mescaline (hallucinogens), and "designer" drugs such as derivatives of fentanyl (a medical narcotic). Precise numbers are not available, but evidence indicates that use is increasing. The "designer" drugs of today will become the "crack" of the 1990s, highly addictive and highly dangerous.

We need to look more closely at the extent of drug abuse among our teenagers, college students, and young adults—they represent our future as a nation. Since 1975, data on drug use in these groups has been monitored by the National Institute on Drug Abuse. This survey is anonymous and is filled out by the respondents themselves. A summary of the 1985 survey follows:[11]

ALCOHOL: Among high-school seniors, 92 percent have tried alcoholic beverages at least once, 66 percent have used alcohol in the last month, 5 percent are using it *daily* and 37 percent admit to an episode of heavy drinking (five drinks or more in a row) within two weeks of being surveyed. Among the college students, daily use is the same at 5 percent. However, heavy drinking is much higher, at 45 percent, and this number increases to 57 percent for the men.

MARIJUANA: Fifty-four percent of all high-school seniors have used pot at least once, 26 percent have used it within the past month, and 5 percent are daily users. Among college students, daily pot use is reported to be only 3.1 percent. These numbers are misleading, however, as Dr. Robert DuPont[12] has found that 40 percent of the 18–21 age group are regular, if not daily, pot smokers.

COCAINE: Cocaine has shown a substantial increase in use despite the adverse press it has received. Seventeen percent of high school seniors have tried it, and 7 percent have used it within the past thirty days. These numbers are the same for the college group. However, use increases dramatically, so that by age 27, 40 percent of young adults have tried cocaine and 10 percent have tried it within the past thirty days.

AMPHETAMINES: Twenty-six percent of high-school seniors have tried them, with 7 percent having used them within the past thirty days. These rates are about half for the college student and young adult groups.

HALLUCINOGENS: (LSD, PCP) Twelve percent of seniors have tried PCP and/or LSD, and 3.5 percent have used them within the past thirty days. Among college students and young adults the reported use is much lower at about 4 percent having tried them and 1 percent using them in the past month.

SEDATIVES/TRANQUILIZERS: These are prescription drugs; however, they are available on the street, and frequently are taken from the parents' medicine cabinet. Twenty-two percent of seniors have tried at least one of these drugs and 4.5 percent have used them in the past thirty days. Among the college and young adult group, only about 6 percent admit to trying these drugs.

The interesting thing about these numbers is that the reported downward trend in drug use, especially of cocaine, by the college and young adult group is not supported by the evidence. We believe that this represents either denial ("I'm just a casual user, and that doesn't count") on the part of those surveyed or the fear that being truthful could jeopardize their education or employment.

A recent study has estimated that drug abuse is costing $50 billion in excess insurance costs.[13] In 1983, according to the National Center for Health Statistics, the direct costs (such as lost work-time, accidents, treatment, hospitalization, legal, assistance, and law enforcement) exceeded $116 billion for alcohol alone. The Center also estimated that the total costs for drug abuse that year were $177 billion. In 1986 the Bureau of National Affairs estimated that alcoholism may cost American businesses as much as $100 billion annually, including medical bills and insurance premiums, productivity losses and business failures.

How do we count the cost of drug and alcohol use? In dollars? In lives lost? In families disrupted? In children abused by intoxicated parents? In years spent in prison? In terms of jobs lost? It is all of these and more. One particularly tragic cost was the recent accidental death of a nine-year-old boy from

COUNSELING FOR SUBSTANCE ABUSE AND ADDICTION ——

cocaine overdose, mentioned in chapter 2. This did not happen
in the big city, but in a rural farm community!

A sixth grade class in Pasadena, California, was listening
to a talk about alcoholism by a staff member of the local
Council on Alcoholism. After the talk, one of the students
who was a promising football player asked: "Will I have to
learn how to drink Lite beer in order to become a pro
football player?"

In the final analysis, however, the major cost is in lives
forever damaged—physically, emotionally, and spiritually.
"Those teenagers who listen to its siren song and succumb to its
inviting lure find that marijuana use is a way to hide out from
pain, to feel that they belong without having to work for real
friendship. They see it as a way to dampen the painful fires of
ambition and shut down goal-driven behaviors; it makes them
feel, 'My world's okay the way it is.' . . . Thanks to pot, their
vision of personal achievement is progressively restricted. Academic goals plummet. Sports and other extracurricular activities requiring work are casually abandoned. Once-cherished
personal goals weaken and vanish. The desire to be married
and have a family, like the ambition for college and a career,
often go [sic] up in puffs of smoke."[14]

CHAPTER FOUR

IF DRUGS ARE SO BAD, WHY DO PEOPLE KEEP USING THEM?

HOW DENIAL AND GUILT PERPETUATE DRUG ABUSE

Peter Skidmore [age 15] was bored. He put down the ball-point pen and closed the blue spiral notebook. Then he reached for the plastic bong [pipe for smoking marijuana] he hid behind his bookcase, the secret place where he had hidden favorite toys as a kid. He tamped down the marijuana, lit a match, closed his lips over the plastic mouthpiece, and inhaled the smoke. He opened the notebook to that day's entry and picked up the pen.

"I can't figure out why I get high because I don't really

enjoy it. I smoke not enough to be escaping life, although to some extent I am. . . . I feel so lost in everything. There seems to be nothing I can hang onto." Peter Skidmore got high three or four times a day. Once before breakfast, once at the break between second and third period, once at lunch, and once again when he got home.

"It kept me company," he says now. "Whenever I needed a break from home, or whenever I was sad or lonely, I'd go down to this bridge in Rock Creek Park near the house and get high."

At school, he'd walk outside to a clearing in the woods, where boys would gather to joke and pass a joint or two. Peter says he never had to buy any marijuana. His friends supplied it. Some grew it in their backyards.

His interest in outside activities began to dwindle. He lived in a state of suspended animation, hardly speaking to his parents. He was irritable. He lied constantly. Bill Skidmore [Peter's father] still thought it might be normal. Teenagers always went through a period of estrangement from their parents.[1]

Peter eventually entered a treatment program and became drug-free. But it took a crisis in his family before his parents admitted to themselves that their son had a drug problem. Then they sought help.

This may be the most difficult of all the chapters in the book to understand. It considers why an otherwise healthy and intelligent human being will systematically poison himself or herself with a drug of abuse. This pattern of mental and spiritual blindness to the real severity of a drug problem in oneself or in someone else is referred to as *denial*.

DENIAL

Denial is most simply defined as not recognizing or admitting a problem, despite the adverse consequences. Denial is a very common behavior, and is the drug abuser's usual way of avoiding unpleasant realities. The use of denial by the drug abuser (and usually by family members, as well) is the primary reason that many people stay dependent on or addicted to drugs for years. If drug abuse is not acknowledged, it will not be dealt with, and it will continue. The underlying attitude behind denial is, "what problem?"

Witness the following story of a former professional athlete and his battles with cocaine use:

> Proclaiming he is not a drug addict, former football star Warren McVea was placed on probation for eight years and fined $4,000 for possessing cocaine. McVea, 40, pleaded guilty and was sentenced by State District Judge Carl Walker, Jr., who asked McVea about his drug problem. "He said he didn't have one," Walker said later. "But that's not what I understand."
>
> Prosecutor Lisa Amos said she was dismayed to hear McVea deny his drug abuse. "He's not going to make it with that attitude," Amos said. McVea was arrested Dec. 18 in the bathroom of a squalid southwest Houston apartment as he and two companions were cooking cocaine to make "crack." He was charged with possessing a vial that contained cocaine residue.[2]

Substance abusers know, on a logical, thought level, that they are hurting themselves and others, but the euphoria (or drug high) is learned within the feeling center of the brain, not in the logical, thinking center. In the face of every reason to stop abusing drugs or alcohol, they continue to abuse, being driven to use the substances by impulses emanating from the feeling center of the brain. The logical center of the brain seems unable to control the intense psychological and physiological craving for the substance of abuse. As one might expect, over a period of time tremendous conflict develops between the thinking and feeling centers of the brain, and, in order to prevent total internal emotional chaos, the mind develops an internal psychological system of defense, the denial system. Although this denial system may protect the mind from the psychological pain of this internal conflict, it unfortunately serves to perpetuate the addiction by allowing substance abusers to deceive themselves and avoid the awareness of the true extent of the addiction. There are at least seven forms of denial which may be called the substance abuser's denial system.

1. *Rationalization* is using a socially acceptable but untrue explanation for inappropriate behavior when acknowledging the real reason would reveal inadequacies and shortcomings in the individual. Substance abusers will always have "good" reasons for their drug-using behavior.

2. *Projection* is the blaming of others for one's own failings and inadequacies. The drug user says that the reason for losing his job is because "the boss didn't like me," when the real reason is poor performance due to drug use. He is suspended from school because the teacher is "out to get" him. These failings also lead to the development of intense hostility and anger, which is then brought home and directed at family and loved ones.

3. *Repression* is the unconscious exclusion from one's conscious mind of unbearable thoughts, experiences, or feelings. This allows one to "forget" the unpleasant events and activities of drug use. Repression leads to a generalized feeling of guilt.

4. *Suppression* is the conscious pushing away of unpleasant feelings and events into the background. Unlike repression, these feelings and events can be recalled at will. Substance abusers suppress feelings and emotions because they do not have healthy coping mechanisms to deal with them. Or, they cover them up with more drugs.

5. *Withdrawal* is the deliberate avoidance of relationships and communication with those around a person. Withdrawal accomplishes two things for the substance abuser. It is a way to avoid intimacy, which allows the drug user to maintain control over others, and it also makes it easier to avoid confrontation about one's drug-using behavior.

6. *Regression* is the reverting of an individual to a level of emotional maturity appropriate to an earlier stage in life. Many adult substance abusers regress to an adolescent level of behavior. When a person begins substance abuse as an adolescent, emotional and psychological development stops and may even reverse to a preadolescent level.

7. *Conversion* is the expression of emotional conflict and feelings through physical symptoms. As used by counselors, it

does not refer to religion. A substance abuser may well be suffering many physical symptoms as a result of drug use. The pain is real, and the individual is truly feeling it. But, it feels worse than it really is because of the conversion mechanism. This allows the drug user to focus on the symptoms and to avoid dealing with the underlying cause, which is his or her drug abuse.

The diagram in Table 2 will help to explain how the denial system can serve to psychologically perpetuate the substance abuser's addiction. Greatly simplified, the brain may be divided into two functional parts, the thinking center and the feeling center. The thinking center is the logical, cognitive area of the brain, where integration and analysis of information takes place and responses are initiated. This center is also responsible for control of voluntary muscle activity.

The feeling center is where emotions originate. It is called the limbic system, and is activated by the feeling center of the brain. "The limbic system controls emotions and motivation. It is made up of a number of centers including the hypothalamus, the amygdala, and the septum. The hypothalamus controls eating and drinking and contains the pleasure centers [where drugs act]. The amygdala and the septum control aggressiveness and emotion."[3]

In order to understand and effectively help the drug abuser, one must appreciate how the denial system of the mind operates. The denial system "protects" the mind from the psychological pain of the intense conflicts which would otherwise occur between the logical, thinking center of the brain and the feeling center. The denial system allows the substance abuser to isolate his or her rational, logical thoughts from feelings. Once the denial system has succeeded in "splitting" the thinking center and the feeling center from one another, then the thinking center is greatly weakened in its ability to monitor and control the impulses of the feeling center. The feeling center is then made very vulnerable to the development of addiction. As seen in Table 2, once the denial system has succeeded in severing clear and truthful communication between the thinking center and the feeling center, then a person's behavior can alternately be controlled by either the thinking center or the feeling center. In a substance abuser, the power of the drug addiction is so strong that the feeling center of the brain often dominates the behavior and controls it, allowing the addictive patterns to continue. We like to think that we are rational, logical beings; however, we frequently live by our feelings. The substance abuser is enslaved by feelings and the associated addiction.

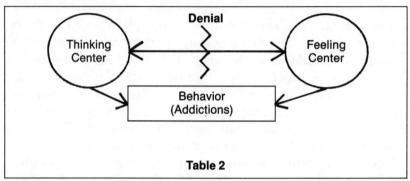

Table 2

The mind's denial system is the great "psychological supporter" of substance abuse. At its core, substance abuse comes or originates from a breakdown in the basic psychological control mechanisms of the mind. Where truth, clarity, and responsibility should exist, denial has taken over; truly things have begun to go wrong within the human machine. C. S. Lewis, the great Christian apologist, offers this insight: "There are two ways in which the human machine goes wrong. One is when human individuals drift apart from one another, or else collide with one another and do one another damage, by cheating or bullying. The other is when things go wrong inside the individual—when the different parts of him (his different faculties and desires and so on) either drift apart or interfere with one another."[4]

The capacity to use a small amount of denial in a healthy fashion was quite likely one of God's original useful capabilities designed for the mind. For example, when a person is able to run into a burning building and rescue someone at great peril to his own safety, he may be exercising healthy denial. Afterward, when asked if he had been afraid, the rescuer will often answer no. Why? Because he was able to deny for a brief time the logical, high likelihood of personal danger, and therefore avoid the fear of personal injury in order to perform the rescue.

In substance abuse, however, we see an example of how the denial system does not perpetuate noble and unselfish behavior. Rather, it actually becomes the major psychological contributor to the continuation of self-destructive substance-abuse patterns.

Although the denial system initially softens the pain and internal anguish of substance abuse, over time, because it is an unnatural psychological system, it requires an increasingly massive amount of emotional energy for it to continue. Eventually, the substance abuser becomes very drained psychologically and can reach the point of being incapable of experiencing—much less processing—day-to-day, normal emotional experiences. Because it is so difficult to maintain this internal, psychological denial system, individuals must develop behavioral "masks" to protect themselves from discovery, disapproval, and deep emotional involvement with others. It is simply a question of internal emotional economics.

So much psychological energy is being absorbed in the process of maintaining the denial system and seeking the drug euphoria that not enough emotional energy is left for healthy, balanced relationships with others. Substance abusers certainly feel a significant amount of loss of control at this point in their lives, and the following behavioral "masks" serve the purpose of attempting to regain some control, protection from the scrutiny of others, and avoidance of burdensome responsibilities. The counselor needs to know and understand these behavioral "masks" if he or she is going to avoid being conned, manipulated, or taken advantage of when attempting to help the substance abuser.

MASKS

Substance abusers also develop attitudes or masks to hide their motives, to rationalize their abnormal behavior, and to deny responsibility for change. They use these masks in order to gain control over the people around them.

The masks of substance abusers include:

- *Closed communication:* Being unwilling to disclose themselves to others, not being receptive to criticism; however, they will criticize themselves as a means of manipulating or conning others.

- *An "I can't" attitude:* This is a common excuse when they are pressed to be responsible. They are quite capable of doing the things that they really want to do.
- *The victim:* This is self-pity, which substance abusers use to deny responsibility for their behavior. They are the "victims" of drugs and cannot help themselves.
- *Lack of time perspective:* Substance abusers have very little concern for the future and especially deny unpleasant results from present behavior. They expect instant results and will frequently drop a task when they can't immediately succeed or achieve immediate gratification.
- *Failure to consider others:* Substance abusers will preserve their self-centeredness by ignoring how their behavior may be hurting others. This allows for a justification of their own behavior, and for them to use and manipulate other people without any concern for their needs or well-being. They are unable to show genuine empathy for others.
- *Avoiding responsibility:* This mask enables substance abusers to avoid responsibility to another individual. As opposed to actively conning or manipulating others, they will also use passivity as a way to avoid responsibility for their behavior.
- *Assumed ownership:* Substance abusers may assume that whatever they want is theirs; their rights transcend those of others. They may be quite possessive toward people they depend upon or have affection for, and they often expect others to do things for them. In their thinking, their illegal activities are not really wrong; they are just a way to secure what "belongs" to them.
- *Denial of bad consequences:* They do not believe that their drug-using behavior is going to harm their health, their family, their job, or their freedom. Ironically, they are often paranoid and frightened by many trivial things.
- *Lack of trust:* Substance abusers are afraid of revealing themselves or trusting themselves to others. They usually demand the trust of others, however.
- *Refusal to be dependent:* They may appear to be dependent

at times, but they are usually doing this to use or manipulate another individual. They are unwilling to be dependent because that means giving up control.

- *Unwilling to be responsible:* They are excellent at "talking a good game," but then fail to follow through on commitments.
- *Pretentiousness:* They believe that the world should treat them as they expect, and not as they deserve. They harbor a deep-seated sense that the world owes them a living and will use their pretentiousness to justify using or taking advantage of others.
- *Unwilling to endure adversity:* They will not endure the struggles of everyday living. However, they will undergo any hardship to obtain and maintain their drug or alcohol supply.

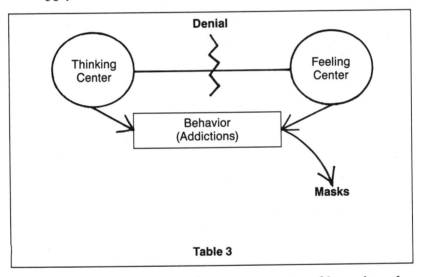

Table 3

Table 3 gives a diagrammatic representation of how the substance abuser proceeds to develop these psychological and behavioral masks as an outgrowth of his or her addiction.

The substance abuser becomes an expert at wearing masks. Paradoxically, because of their continued drug use, addicts cannot consistently maintain this masking behavior. When their defenses are down, they become angry with themselves—angry that they can't stop, angry that they are hurting themselves and those around them, and frequently angry at God for "allowing" them to get into such a mess in the first place. This state of angry frustration and hopelessness becomes so intense that inevitably one major emotion begins to break through the abuser's denial system. That emotion is one of the most powerful and potentially most damaging—*guilt.*

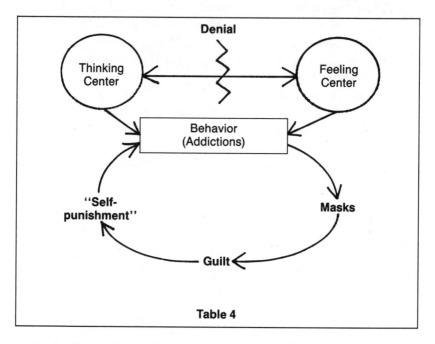

Table 4

Guilt always demands some type of punishment or resolution. Because the denial system has so distorted the substance abuser's ability to deal properly with an emotion as strong as guilt, proper resolution of the guilt almost never occurs. Therefore, guilt begins to serve the extremely negative function of perpetuating self-punishment. The "best" way in which substance abusers can punish themselves is, ironically, to continue to use drugs. This desire for self-punishment is subconscious and not due to their dull, intoxicated state. Soon they become trapped in a cycle. As more *guilt* is produced by the destructive nature of the addiction, more *self-punishment* is called for. Table 4 gives a summary diagrammatic representation of how this cyclical process of *addiction* can lead to behavioral masks, how the *behavioral masks* break down, leaving the individual to deal with guilt, and how *guilt* then proceeds to intensify the need for self-punishment. Finally, the need for *self-punishment* finds its "fulfillment" in the intensification of the addiction. The whole process cycles over again and again.

> Suzie grew up in an average middle-class family. A wife and the mother of three children, she became an alcoholic as an adult. After about two years, she sought treatment in a Christian-oriented program, and began to detoxify.
>
> While in treatment, she committed her life to Christ, began to study the Bible for the first time, learned how to pray and received counseling. Her life began to change and she found happiness that alcohol could never give. Unfortunately, shortly after she finished her detoxification, she relapsed and began drinking again. She felt so guilty (about it and her failures as a parent), that she withdrew from the program and is still drinking.

It is ironic that guilt usually motivates the substance abuser *toward* continued drug use rather than *away* from it. If the cycle of substance abuse is going to be broken, guilt must be dealt with effectively.

Appropriate guilt is the guilt which the substance abuser perceives in response to the unhealthy destructive behaviors carried out while under the influence of the substance. This appropriate guilt can be dealt with by the spiritual and psychological work to be done in the twelve-step process outlined in chapter 7.

David, the psalmist, though not a drug user, struggled with guilt as intensely as any addict ever has. He eloquently describes his struggle in Psalm 32:3–5:

> When I kept silent,
>   my bones wasted away
>   through my groaning all day long.
> For day and night

> your hand was heavy upon me;
>   my strength was sapped
>   as in the heat of summer.
> Then I acknowledged my sin to you
>   and did not cover up my iniquity.
> I said, "I will confess
>   my transgressions to the Lord"—
> and you forgave
>   the guilt of my sin.

Inappropriate guilt, on the other hand, is that guilt which the substance abuser will ironically choose to hold onto in order to maintain the addiction cycle. This guilt is inappropriate, not because it has no basis in fact, but because it is actually a tool the substance abuser utilizes to generate more feelings of self-punishment and, therefore, further intensify the need to "sentence" himself or herself to more intense drug addiction. This inappropriate guilt needs to be pointed out by the counselor and reflected back to the substance abuser. Events in the past cannot be changed, but any real guilt for those events can be erased through the forgiveness available from God through the grace of Jesus Christ. Any remaining inappropriate "need" for the emotion of guilt can then be confronted in the therapeutic process of recovery. *Inappropriate guilt,* and the internal psychological *denial system* make up the sinister "one-two punch" that serves to keep substance abusers addicted for years and years.

You may be asking, "How can I help with all of this going on?" The answer is found in confronting the abuser's denial system. The next chapter tells you how.

CHAPTER FIVE

HELPING IS NOT HELPING

WHY LOVE MUST BE "TOUGH" AND NOT "SOFT"

DEAR ANN LANDERS: We are the parents of a former drug addict, thirty-one years old. As such, I am qualified to offer advice to those troubled parents who wrote of their nineteen-year-old pot smoker. You gave them good advice, Ann, when you said, "Get counseling." I hope they listen. We had to take a very bold and difficult step and let our son know the next time he landed in the hospital, strung out from drugs, he would remain there until he could be placed in a rehab center.

I told him he would not be brought home by loving parents and continue to make their lives hell. Why would anyone want to stay in a rehab center when he could live in a comfortable home, do as he pleases, have no responsibilities and enjoy all the comforts of life? Although we visited our son often and took him out for dinner, we let him know he was not welcome in our home.

After several years of counseling and medication to repair his damaged nervous system, our son has finally emerged from the fog and is now functioning. He returned to college, holds a part-time job and still lives in the rehab house. He would never have come this far if we had continued to pamper him at home, making life easy, allowing him to torture us with his unpredictable, crazy behavior. When we got tough, he got better.—BEEN THROUGH IT IN DETROIT.[1]

These parents have learned the hard way that you cannot help someone who is a drug addict. The addict will only take advantage of the situation, and the addiction will get worse and not better.

What then will help the drug user make the decision to get off drugs and seek treatment? The answer is both profound and yet simple—*pain!* The basic motivation for human change is pain. This pain may be physical, emotional, or spiritual; however, once pain gets our attention we will do something to remove it. Pain in the drug user's life might be the loss of a job, being arrested, severe illness, self-disgust, separation from spouse and children, rejection by family and friends, or something else.

The drug user can temporarily cover up the pain with more drugs. But sooner or later he or she will have to find a workable answer. C. S. Lewis put it this way. "But pain insists upon being attended to. God whispers to us in our pleasures, speaks in our conscience, but shouts in our pains: it is HIS megaphone to rouse a deaf world."[2]

HELPING IS NOT HELPING

How then can you help the drug addict? Don't get in the way of the pain. It may not be easy to stand back and watch as the consequences take their toll, but if you really love the person you must.

Linda Morgan was a loyal wife. When her husband, John, . . . was thrown in jail for public drunkenness, she bailed him out. When he was injured in a drunk-driving accident, she paid the hospital bills and fixed the car. She cleaned up after him when he was sick, put him to bed when he passed out, made up stories to tell his customers when he failed to show up for an auction. Although she was painfully embarrassed when John arrived drunk at his son's Little League game, she never allowed her children to complain about their father. . . .

Over the years, Linda began to pay a physical and emotional price for her husband's unpredictable behavior. She had headaches and high blood pressure. Sometimes she was so depressed she was unable to get out of bed in the morning. She had no emotional energy for spending time with her children, and she felt increasingly tense and angry. . . .

Linda's inability to control either herself or her husband's drinking left her with a deep sense of guilt and failure. Her despair reached suicidal levels, and in desperation she began attending Al-Anon meetings.

At Al-Anon, Linda learned that she was not alone. There were millions of men and women married to alcoholics who felt and behaved just as she did. Her life had become unmanageable, but there was hope. The first step was to accept responsibility for her own actions. The second step was to let John accept responsibility for his.

"It was such a relief to hear that I didn't *cause* John's drinking, I couldn't *control* it, and I couldn't *cure* it," remembers Linda. "But it was months before I was willing to face my own faults. I was so used to blaming everything on John, my spiritual maturity had come to a standstill."

As Linda learned to surrender her life to God, she was able to let John take responsibility for his own life. She still remembers the night she finally gave John to the

Lord. "It was 6:30 in the evening, John was late, and I was praying at the window. Usually I prayed with one eye shut and one eye open, telling God what to do. This time I told God that whatever happened I would praise him. The burden I had been carrying for years left me right there at the window, and I went to fix dinner for the children."

John called late that evening. He had been arrested *at 6:30* and now needed Linda to post bail. Linda told John she loved him. "For the first time in years, I really meant it," Linda says. She also told John that she would not be coming to bail him out. She was sorry he had gotten himself into a mess, but now he would have to get himself out.[3]

Trying to be loving, supportive, and caring of the drug addict usually only makes the situation worse. Concern and compassion shown by friends and loved ones will be taken advantage of, and will ultimately cause harm to the drug user, as well as anger and disillusionment in those doing the helping. Why is this so?

When persons become addicted to drugs they regress emotionally, and can become very immature. They also have to learn how to manipulate, to con, and to lie if they are to be "successful" as addicts. In fact, the addict becomes so good at this that the non-drug user usually does not know that he or she has been taken until after the fact. Their stories, problems, and excuses sound so good that we want to believe them.

Carol got into drugs as a teenager and continued as a young adult. This happened despite her regular church attendance and even teaching Sunday school. Eventually she became addicted to cocaine.

She lived with her widowed father and was supported by him. Despite her being able to work, he did not expect her to because she said that she could not get a job.

She eventually entered treatment. As a part of treatment, her counselor insisted that she get a job, be self-supporting, and live on her own. Carol's father continued to support her and was unwilling to hold her accountable for her behavior. The counselor's goals were never achieved. She dropped out of treatment and is still using drugs.

"Funnel" of Loving Confrontation

Drug users have different levels of tolerance for pain. For some the pain of knowing that they have hurt and disappointed someone they love is enough to motivate them to seek treatment. Unfortunately, others must go all the way to the point of "crash and burn" before they are ready for help.

Confrontation is the process whereby drug-using behavior is acknowledged by others and fully exposed. Accountability and behavior change are expected. "Hating the sin, but loving the sinner," is what is called for. According to Proverbs 27:5, "Better is open rebuke than hidden love." Neither preaching nor holding up a standard of behavior will accomplish the objective. If the counselor wants to see someone become drug-free, he or she must be tough, despite the person's resistance.

A progression of steps can be followed in trying to encourage the drug abuser to seek treatment. These may take place over a period of months, or years. However, the progression may be much shorter—weeks or months—especially when dealing with adolescents. Frequently the first three steps will need to be utilized simultaneously. We call this *the funnel of loving confrontation.*

A good example of this type of confrontation is presented in 2 Samuel 12. It occurred between the prophet, Nathan, and King David concerning David's adultery with Bathsheba and his murder of her husband. Apparently Nathan gave David time to deal with the situation. Though David chose not to, Nathan did not withdraw from their relationship. God kept putting the heat on David, as recorded in Psalm 32.

Finally, after more than a year had passed, Nathan raised the issue with David. He did not preach at David or condemn him, but laid out the facts of the situation. David responded by acknowledging his wrongdoing. There was no argument, no denying the facts, and no excuse-making. Verse 13 states: "Then David said to Nathan, 'I have sinned against the Lord.'" Nathan spoke to David, not out of the anger of the moment, but objectively stating the facts. This is a key point to remember: we shouldn't, as counselors, get drawn into arguing and shouting. If necessary, we should say what we have to say later, when we are not angry and when we can lay out our facts or feelings 'objectively.

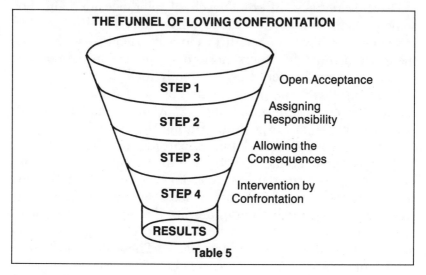

THE FUNNEL OF LOVING CONFRONTATION

STEP 1 — Open Acceptance

STEP 2 — Assigning Responsibility

STEP 3 — Allowing the Consequences

STEP 4 — Intervention by Confrontation

RESULTS

Table 5

Step 1: Open Acceptance

This step works on the principle that the drug abuser must be drawn into the process of positive change. This open acceptance is based on his or her need for a relationship with a *significant other*. "Significant other" refers to the person (there is often more than one) who has a close personal relationship with the drug user—a relationship the drug user values and does not want to lose.

This person is usually a family member, but he or she may also be a close friend, an employer, a co-worker, or a fellow church member. Whomever it may be, the key is that the drug user cares what that individual thinks about him or her and wants to continue the relationship.

The objective is not for anyone to confront the substance abuser yet, but simply to become "indispensable" in the right kind of way, developing an open acceptance of him or her as a person, viewing the person as someone worthy of love. This love is based upon the needs of the abuser, and not on the abuser's behavior. You, or the "significant other," are not condoning the behavior, and may need to say so.

Step 2: Assigning Responsibility

Assigning responsibility to the substance abuser for the consequences of the behavior is the next step in the ever-tightening funnel. The person who is the "significant other" quits making excuses for the drug user's behavior and actions. Rationalizations and excuses are no longer accepted. The substance abuser is expected to take responsibility, and to be accountable for his or her behavior.

The drug abuser will resist taking this responsibility and will come up with even more excuses or reasons for what problems exist, and they will all sound plausible at first. However, the truth will eventually become apparent. Chapter 4 details the attitudes that are part of this resistance and denial of responsibility.

Step 3: Allowing the Consequences

As the "funnel" constricts even further, the substance abuser will regularly plead with the significant people in his or her environment for rescue from the increasingly painful consequences of drug-related behavior. The "significant other" who has decided to enforce this funnel of loving confrontation must take a loving, but firm, stand.

At this point the drug user may be agreeable to treatment. If so, then you need to have options ready to present. Failing to plan is planning to fail. Chapter 9 will help you decide which type of treatment would be best to recommend to the person directly involved with the drug abuser.

Here are some practical guidelines for the "significant other," to help him or her put these first three steps into action.

Get the facts

Become informed about drugs and alcohol and their effects. Know who the drug user is associating with, maintaining as good a relationship with him or her as possible while doing so. If the substance abuser is a teenager or young adult, make it your business to know who the person's friends are, and who the parents are. Don't be afraid to communicate with the parents, asking questions so that you know specifics of when and where drug use is occurring.

Stand your ground

Make your position on drugs and alcohol clear so that the substance abuser knows where you stand, even if you do not know the total extent of the drug use. Be prepared to defend your position in as rational a manner as is possible.

Be united

Be sure that the significant individuals in the drug user's life are in agreement about how to deal with the drug abuse. You need to demonstrate *consistency* and *mutual support.*

Keep your expectations high

Let the substance abuser know that the behavior you are expecting from him or her may be different from that of the person's peers and friends. Make it clear that certain behaviors are unacceptable, and explain what the consequences will be for those behaviors. You will need to be firm, and will sometimes seem harsh in enforcing this.

Keep your cool

Avoid unsupported accusations, name-calling, or a personal attack ("You're no good! You're just like your father!"). These will simply result in denial. Let the drug abuser know how you feel without being overly emotional. Avoid angry outbursts as these only serve to cut off communication.

Be prepared to follow through

Make sure you are prepared to follow through with the conditions and consequences that you have set. Empty threats are meaningless and will be put to the test. Giving in to the drug abuser at this critical stage may help prolong the person's drug use, and postpone the decision to get help.

The following letter will clarify the points we have just made.

I am an alcoholic. I need help.

Don't allow me to lie to you and accept it for the truth, for in so doing, you encourage me to lie. The truth may be painful, but get at it.

Don't let me outsmart you. This only teaches me to avoid responsibility and to lose respect for you at the same time.

Don't let me exploit you or take advantage of you. In so doing, you become an accomplice to my evasion of responsibility.

Don't lecture me, moralize, scold, praise, blame, or argue when I'm drunk or sober. And don't pour out my liquor; you may feel better, but the situation will be worse.

Don't accept my promises. This is just my method of postponing pain. And don't keep switching agreements. If an agreement is made, stick to it.

Don't lose your temper with me. It will destroy you and any possibility of helping me.

Don't allow your anxiety for us to compel you to do what I must do for myself.

Don't cover up or abort the consequences of my drinking. It reduces the crisis but perpetuates the illness.

Above all, don't run away from reality as I do. Alcoholism, my illness, gets worse as my drinking continues. Start now to learn, to understand, and to plan for my recovery. I need help from a doctor, a counselor, a psychologist, a recovered alcoholic, from God. I cannot help myself.

I hate myself, but I love you. To do nothing is the worst choice you can make for us.

Step 4: Intervention by Confrontation

Finally, if the first three steps fail to convince the drug user of the need for help, a direct confrontation along with intervention will be necessary. This is done to convince the substance abuser of the effects of destructive behavior (on both the person and his or her family) and confront the abuser with the mandate for getting treatment.

1. Intervention—why and how. Usually the drug user has to hit bottom before he or she is willing to get help. Unfortunately, while waiting for things to get worse, they indeed do.

COUNSELING FOR SUBSTANCE ABUSE AND ADDICTION ────

This can lead to irreversible consequences, such as suicide, an overdose, permanent damage to health, or the loss of family. Fortunately, the process of reaching the bottom can be speeded up or precipitated by the technique known as *intervention*. This is both a process (a how) and an event (a what); it is both the preparation for, and presentation of a loving confrontation. During this confrontation, substance abusers are told: (1) the harmful effects of their behavior on themselves and their loved ones and (2) the consequences of continuing their drug lifestyle. Then (3) they are offered treatment for the addiction.

Hank was a good manager. Five years ago, he began entertaining his business associates with the "three martini" lunch. His drinking extended after work and his alcohol intake increased to the point that he was getting drunk two or three times weekly. He started missing work.

Once active in community and church activities, he withdrew from everything. His teenage children were ashamed to bring friends home for fear of his behavior and appearance. His wife, a loving woman, was at her "wit's end." She spoke with their pastor who referred her to a local treatment center. Hank refused to go, but she went.

She began attending Al-Anon and learned about alcoholism and its effects on the entire family. Working with her pastor and a substance-abuse counselor, Hank's wife prepared for an intervention. Additionally, their pastor, the couple's teenagers, and Hank's parents all prepared to participate.

They met with Hank one Friday morning. The intervention went well, with each one present sharing how he or she had experienced the impact of Hank's drinking. Hank entered treatment that afternoon. After intensive therapy and counseling, he is sober, functional, and happy today.

2. The process. *First,* gain as much knowledge as you can about the problem. Resources are listed in Appendix 3 of this book. Find as much written material as you can. Locate your local support groups such as Al-Anon, Nar-Anon, Toughlove, Families Anonymous, Parents Against Drugs, and attend their

meetings. The support and encouragement will help you and those you counsel follow through. Contact hospitals which have substance-abuse treatment programs.

Second, direct the family to gather together (without the abuser) and discuss how the abuser's behavior affects their lives. Have them describe who else has been affected, such as an employer, employees, neighbors, friends, and others. Ask the counselee if these individuals might be invited to participate in the intervention.

Third, investigate local treatment options, both inpatient and outpatient programs. Be sure you check the cost, insurance coverage, and types of programs offered. Chapter 9 contains a summary of the different types of treatment available, and indicates which is usually the most appropriate.

Fourth, consult with your peers in the substance-abuse field if you lack the expertise. They can assist you with the intervention process and event. If need be, they can facilitate the actual intervention so that it is coupled with an appropriate treatment plan and program.

Be sure your goals for the intervention are clear to everyone. Here are some to consider:

(a) To secure the drug user's agreement to become drug free.

(b) To get the person's agreement and commitment to a plan for accomplishing this. This would include a change of behavior and habits.

(c) To decide which type of treatment program would be best.

Rehearsal is vital to a successful intervention. One individual needs to act as the facilitator of the event. This may be you, the counselor; or it may be some other professional, or an experienced layperson, a family member, a close friend of the abuser, or an employer. Each participant needs to practice how and what they will say to the abuser. They are counseled to state only facts about how the abuser's behavior has affected them personally, and not to preach, teach, or chastise. Available options for behavioral change and treatment should be discussed with the professionals involved in coordinating the event.

3. The event. The family and others assemble before the

substance abuser arrives. The facilitator should speak first and act as the moderator, explaining to the substance abuser why they have gathered and asking him or her to listen without responding for a while. Each person then speaks directly with the substance abuser, sharing facts, events, and personal reactions to the abuser's behavior, and telling how it has affected each. This is an objective attack on the drug user's denial system, not on the person.

Possible options for help are shared. Then the abuser is allowed to respond. Responses vary from a complete denial of any problem to a tearful acceptance of the need to seek professional help. The group should be prepared for other responses including anger, hostility, and counter-accusations, as well as the possibility of the abuser bolting from the room.

It is vital that when a decision has been made, follow-up action taken is immediate and consistent. The drug user must not be allowed to bargain with the group or postpone entering treatment. The facilitator may even need a court order mandating treatment against the user's will. Twenty-four hours may be too long to wait for that may provide the user enough time to develop new excuses and rationalizations for the behavior, allowing him or her to deny the facts presented during the intervention.

Whatever the response, the facilitator must be sure the message is clearly delivered: "You can continue to destroy yourself, but we will no longer assist you in that process. You are responsible for your own actions, and their consequences." The group *must* be prepared to mean business and to follow through, no matter how difficult that may be for both the drug user and those in the group. The following are guidelines the counselor can share with the group and the family to help them deal with the abuser.

KEYS TO DEALING WITH THE DRUG ABUSER
DON'T

- do anything until you gather the facts that you need.
- attempt to punish, threaten, bribe, or preach. (This will only raise defense mechanisms higher.)

- use emotional appeals which perpetuate the guilt-punishment cycle.
- soft-pedal the issues and ignore the events.
- assume the roles and tasks the abuser is neglecting.
- argue with the substance abuser while he or she is under the influence.
- cover up for, make excuses for, or rescue the substance abuser from the consequences of drug use.
- hide or throw out the substance of abuse until you have informed the abuser that you are going to do so.
- use drugs along with the addict.
- accept guilt for the abuser's behavior.

DO

- let the substance abuser know you care for him or her, but you don't condone the actions.
- learn about drug and alcohol abuse by reading, getting professional advice, and attending support group meetings.
- discuss the situation with someone you trust.
- let the substance abuser know the effects of his or her behavior on you.
- maintain a healthy atmosphere in the home, continuing with day-to-day activities of living. (Don't forsake your needs because of the abuser.)
- explain the nature of addiction as discussed herein to the children in words they can understand.
- remember to be patient and live one day at a time. Recovery from drug abuse is a lifelong process.

CHAPTER SIX

ADDICTION IS A FAMILY AFFAIR

THE DESTRUCTIVE EFFECTS OF DRUG ABUSE
ON THE ENTIRE FAMILY

As professional counselors, David and Phyllis York had some success with other people's children, not much with their own. Five years ago, police in Lansdale, Pa., showed up at the York house with shotguns and a warrant for their 18-year-old daughter. The charge: holding up a cocaine dealer. Says David York, 52: "It hit me that my kids were really going bonkers on us and there had to be something better we could do." So the Yorks founded Toughlove, an association of anxious parents who were dedicated to drawing the line against out-of-control youngsters and forcing them to behave.[1]

The Yorks discovered firsthand that drug abuse and its related harmful behavior adversely affect the entire family, not just the drug user. Frequently, the behavior and attitudes of parents, grandparents, siblings, or spouses toward the drug user will enable or encourage him or her to continue using drugs, rather than to seek treatment. Conversely, the attitudes and behavior of the drug user will be detrimental to the lives of the nonusing family members. Fortunately, rather than denying the problem or blaming each other, the Yorks implemented a decisive plan of action.

It has been said that the substance abuser lives in a world with a population of one—one's self. Being inner-directed and virtually absorbed with one's own pain or pleasure makes even the most congenial substance abuser a very self-centered person.

This self-centeredness is not just an unfortunate personality trait. It impairs normal, day-to-day living and interpersonal relationships. A pattern of behavior emerges that is both disruptive and destructive to the entire family. A marriage in which one partner is a drug or alcohol abuser has a one-in-ten chance of survival.

It is estimated that each alcoholic adversely affects four other persons. Most commonly, those persons are his or her own family members. Since there are an estimated 12 million alcoholics in the United States, there are approximately 48 million additional victims of alcoholism. This includes 20 million adults who have grown up in alcoholic families and 7 million children who are still being raised in alcoholic families. Millions more are in families of those hooked on other drugs.

Recognizing the problems that the whole family can have because of drug abuse, and getting help for the entire family, not just the user, is crucial to successful treatment. The following letter puts it very well.

I am the father who wrote you about drug testing for his son. On your advice I had a urinalysis done and my son tested positive for marijuana and methamphetamine. I want to thank you for your advice. So does my son.

He is now in a drug rehabilitation program. Our whole family, including my wife and our two younger children, is in counseling to help each other with the problems that led to this situation.[2]

PULVERIZATION OF THE FAMILY UNIT

Living in the family of the drug or alcohol user is like being on the wrong side of a two-headed coin—you can never win. The only thing constant in the home is the inconsistency and unpredictability. The parent or teen who is addicted is one minute pleasant and loving, the next full of anger and hostility.

Being in a no-win situation brings out certain behaviors and habit patterns that are very abnormal, but necessary for survival. This is called codependency and is discussed more fully in chapter 8. If both the user and the user's family enter treatment this can usually be reversed. Unfortunately, in many families no treatment is sought. If a parent is the user, the children suffer the most. This is understandably worse if both parents abuse drugs. When children of such a home become adults, they frequently feel worthless and have great difficulty with close, intimate relationships. Conway Hunter, Jr., M.D., a physician in private practice in Atlanta, Georgia, in his contribution to the book *The Courage to Change,* states, "You show me your child of an alcoholic and I'll show you a sick child."

The tremendous emotional scars inflicted upon children growing up in alcoholic homes lead directly to marital discord, emotional depression, vocational instability, and job dissatisfaction in adulthood.

Marie grew up in a family in which both of her parents were alcoholics. She was frequently beaten by her mother. Her family never sought treatment. As a teenager she started using pain pills and tranquilizers. By age 18 she was addicted to heroin.

She entered a Christian treatment program, gave her life over to God, and eventually became drug-free. However, life has been anything but easy. In spite of having a supportive husband and a beautiful, loving child, even though she is drug-free, Marie struggles with a great sense of rejection and acts in ways to get rejected (this was the way her parents treated her as a child).

Characteristic behavior traits and attitudes plague the children of the alcohol and drug user. These begin in childhood and continue into adulthood. These have been identified and described beautifully by Janet Woititz in her book *Adult Children of Alcoholics*. They include:

- The children are confused as to what "normal" is.
- They have difficulty completing projects or tasks.
- They lie compulsively, even when there is no need to.
- They are overly critical of themselves.
- They take themselves too seriously and have difficulty having fun.
- As adults they have difficulty with intimate relationships.
- There is a great need for control of one's life, and excessive anger when this cannot be achieved.
- There is a life-long need for approval and affirmation.
- There is a feeling of being different from other people.
- They are either overly responsible or overly irresponsible.
- There is extreme loyalty to the abuser even though it is unwarranted.
- There is frequent impulsive behavior which only aggravates the existing problems.[3]

Bea is a young adult who has problems with depression and a feeling of worthlessness. Both of her parents were alcoholics. After years of struggling with these feelings, she sought help through Adult Children of Alcoholics. She said: "It's only been recently that I realized that our family problems were due to my parents' alcoholism. I always thought that there was something wrong with me."

Dr. Hunter's research also shows that nine out of ten times the daughter of an alcoholic father will marry an alcoholic. He believes that she becomes so accustomed to an inappropriate caretaking role, that when she grows up she looks for someone, usually unconsciously, with the same pitiful neediness of her own father. This is also associated with a high incidence of physical abuse by the alcoholic husband. In fact, it has been stated that repeated spouse abuse is virtually nonexistent without the involvement of drugs or alcohol.

When a member of the family is regularly using drugs or alcohol, the family may often feel as if it's living with a time bomb. The family experiences great swings between periods of emotional outburst and periods of withdrawal, all the while waiting uneasily for the next crisis to occur. Fears of violence, embarrassment, serious illness, and even suicide or overdose permeate the family.

Family members often describe living in such a home as existing between the two extremes of crisis mobilization and hopeless despair. In between the two there are short "calm" periods when the family waits for the next crisis to occur, much as a storm survivor in the eye of a hurricane apprehensively waits out the uneasy and transient calm for the next blast of the hurricane's fury.

The Substance Abuser

The lives of substance abusers are motivated largely by a sense of shame and inadequacy—shame over their choice of using a chemical crutch, and inadequacy in that they cannot find another way to cope with the pressures of life and the world around them. The payoff of their addiction is relief of emotional pain and guilt, and the defense which they use is denial—denial of the seriousness of the problem, denial of the impact of the problem on family and friends, and denial of the inevitable downward course of their lives.

The price the substance abusers pay is the destruction of their own health and self-esteem. It is also paid by those individuals around them who are dragged—emotionally, spiritually, and sometimes physically—with them into the pitiful abyss of their addiction.

ROLES IN THE SUBSTANCE-ABUSE FAMILY

The anguish of family members in the home of a substance abuser drives them into certain roles which they adopt in order to survive the chaos.[4] These roles are generally not healthy, but they are, in a sense, protective. That is, they allow the substance abuser and his or her family to develop a means of coping with the incredible emotional stress infecting the home. The chart on page 98 describes six roles that characteristically are found in the substance-abuse family.

The Enabler

This is a role that is usually undertaken by some key person in the substance abuser's immediate family (spouse or parent), or by a close friend. The *enabler* feels compelled to try, at all costs, to decrease the chaos which the drug use is producing. However, in doing so, he or she only helps perpetuate the addiction. Without an enabler, it would be hard for the user to continue the habit.

Understandably, the primary feeling which the enabler develops is anger, although it is oftentimes covered by a veneer of concern and patient unselfishness. He or she often overprotects and tries to rescue the substance abuser, and will not let the user suffer the consequences of the addiction. The payoff is peace at any cost.

Bob is a successful executive and a supportive and caring husband. His wife is addicted to prescription tranquilizers and has no intention of giving them up. In addition to his job, Bob takes care of the house and the children. He recently went for counseling and was advised that the only way his wife would be willing to change would be for him and the children to move out. His reply to his counselor was, "I'm a Christian, and I could never leave her or hurt her." Bob continues in the role of both "husband" and "wife." His wife continues to lie in bed, day in and day out, and take her pills.

There are generally four types of enablers. The classic scenario of the alcoholic husband and the enabling wife affords an excellent opportunity to look at the four types. However, all combinations of parent, spouse, child, grandparent, boyfriend/girlfriend, employer, and drug user exist.

The Sufferer. The sufferer tries to change her alcoholic husband by showing him that he is really hurting her with his addiction. She may suffer physically and develop various ailments; she may suffer socially and make it clear to him that she is embarrassed by his behavior; or she may suffer quietly by simply exuding a constant air of self-pity and martyrdom.

The Punisher. The punisher tries to change her husband by making his life absolutely miserable. Unfortunately, she tends to punish when she is particularly frustrated or humiliated by his drug-using behavior. There is no consistent enforcement of responsibility, but rather an intermittent lashing out both verbally and sometimes physically. This behavior does not serve to reduce drug use, but only leads to his becoming more cunning and deceptive in hiding and minimizing it.

The Controller. The controller tries to reduce her husband's addiction by systematically controlling and supervising every possible area of his life. Controllers often make phone calls to check up on their spouses and frequently enlist the help of friends, fellow church members, and co-workers to monitor his behavior. These efforts at control only increase his sense of frustration and resentment.

The Waverer. The waverer is one who tries to intervene and reduce the alcohol use of her spouse. Unfortunately, the intense perseverance and the emotional toughness that must accompany these interventions is not long-lived. She wanes in her capacity to "keep the heat on" and force him to follow through with responsible behavior. When she wavers, her substance-abusing spouse takes that opportunity to return to full-blown addiction.

The Family Hero

This is the individual who believes that somehow, directly or indirectly, he or she is responsible for the substance abuser's addiction. This guilt is usually false, yet the family hero feels it just the same. For example, if a child thinks that his father's alcoholism has worsened because he was not able to "make daddy proud" by achievements at school, he may become driven toward super achievement. By achieving, the child believes he may help reverse the problem, and make Dad feel better.

The characteristic behavior of the family hero is overachievement. The personality defense this person uses most often is obsessive, compulsive behavior which reduces the world to a set of black and white absolutes—victory or defeat—all or none, etc. The payoff for the family hero is positive attention and praise, and a boost in the person's sense of self-worth. He or she may try vainly to please the drug-using parent and to impress the world that all is well with the family, but the price which the family hero usually pays is eventual workaholism; the family hero bases his or her self-worth on performance. "Achieve or leave" is this person's motto.

> Sue grew up with an alcoholic mother. Her mother blamed her for her alcoholism. Sue herself also felt responsible for her mother's addiction. Though she was the youngest child in her family, she excelled in school and accomplished far more than her older siblings. Years later, she is now married to a successful physician, has two beautiful children, and is one of the leading women in her church. Despite this, and knowing God's love, she still feels a great sense of inadequacy and always thinks that she must try harder to please others.

The Scapegoat

The scapegoat in the family feels damaged or inferior, often like a victim. And since this person perceives himself or herself as damaged and unwanted, he or she may decide that attention for being "bad" is better than no attention at all. Delinquent and rebellious behavior is common, along with frequent criminal activity.

The scapegoat's defense against emotional pain is substitution. This person will substitute anything that can be found as relief for the pain of being "a loser." For example, the scapegoat may withdraw from the family and look solely toward peers as a source of approval. Scapegoats are often easy prey for cults, or the latest fad in dress and music and drugs, or "the wrong crowd," as they clamor incessantly for attention and a sense of belonging. Their deep sense of rejection leads them to seek the payoff of attention, even if this attention is negative. The price that the scapegoat pays is alienation from normal living.

Melanie grew up in a very affluent and socially prominent family. Both of her parents drank heavily. Melanie felt that she would never be allowed to be her own person. She found as a teenager that drugs provided an escape. By the time she graduated from high school, she was well-known to her peers as a "druggie." She continued using drugs until age 32, when she was hospitalized to treat her withdrawal symptoms. She entered counseling and committed her life to Christ. Though she is still struggling, she is now drug-free and has found real happiness for the first time in her life.

The Lost Child

This family member withdraws from the family in a quiet way, but not in an openly defiant way as the scapegoat does. Loneliness is the most common feeling of the "lost child," who is often quiet and passive. This one is willing to "go with the flow" and to use emotional and physical retreat as a defense against the painful events occurring in the home.

The payoff for the lost child is to escape from the home's chaos into his or her own little world where tranquillity can be enforced. This escape tactic also, at times, diverts attention away from the substance abuser. Large amounts of emotional energy, time, and money are focused on the lost child in an effort to "bring him out of his shell."

Karen was the third of five children. Her mother was an alcoholic. Karen was a quiet child and rarely caused trouble. When she left home for college, finding that she had difficulty in forming close relationships, she herself turned to alcohol for solace and companionship. Ten years passed before she sought treatment.

The Mascot

The mascot is the family clown or joker. This person fears that the chaos at home will suddenly reach a boiling point and explode. This uneasiness at home causes the mascot to use humor and superficiality as a diversion to cheer up the dreary and depressing atmosphere.

Roles in the Substance Abusing Family

The Person	The Feeling	The Behavior	Defense Mechanism	Payoff	Price	Parental Message
Drug abuser	Shame	Addiction (dependence)	Denial	Relief of emotional pain	Personal destruction	"Don't do like I'm doing, because you are just like me."
Enabler	Anger and helplessness	Worry and over-protection or lashing out in anger	Avoidance	Peace (temporary)	Self-deception and perpetuation of addiction	"What Dad did was terrible, but remember, he was an alcoholic."
Family hero	False guilt	Over achievement	Obsessive-compulsive and rigid behavior	Positive attention and increased self-esteem	Workaholism and burnout	"It's your successes that make my life bearable."
Scapegoat	Damaged (inferior)	Delinquent, rebellious behavior	Substitution	Negative attention and acceptance (wrong peers)	Rejection and alienation	"If you would stop causing trouble, things would be OK."
Lost child	Loneliness	Passive behavior (personal camouflage)	Retreat	Escape	Social isolation	"I love you. Now go away."
Mascot (clown or joker)	Fear of catastrophe	Joking, clowning, overactive, excessively helpful	Diversion	Relief of fear	Immaturity	"You're cute (entertaining) but not important."

Table 6

Those who are mascots often succeed in relieving the dread of catastrophe for a short while, but their chronic joking and antics can be carried into adulthood, resulting in emotional immaturity. Some of Hollywood's greatest entertainers and comedians have come from substance-abusing homes where they developed the role of mascot or clown in an effort to offset the otherwise oppressive and painful atmosphere. Their motto is "loved by all, known by none."

> Both of Gail's parents were alcoholics. Gail found that she had a naturally quick wit. She also found that her humor provided comic relief and helped defuse the hostility that existed in the household.
> Fortunately she did not follow her parents into addiction as her sister and brother did. Gail is now working as a substance-abuse counselor. She describes herself as a workaholic. She is working on establishing greater intimacy between herself, her husband, and her children.

Your role as a counselor is to assist the family in identifying what roles the members have played in the family system. This may not be easy, as they may well be using denial and believe that only the substance abuser has a problem. If they can acknowledge their roles and then get help themselves they can become part of the solution instead of remaining part of the problem.

CHAPTER SEVEN

THE ROAD TO RECOVERY

WHAT IT TAKES TO GET OUT OF ADDICTION

King Heroin is my shepherd, I shall always want.
He maketh me to lie down in the gutters.
He leadeth me beside the troubled waters.
He destroyeth my soul.
He leadeth me in the paths of wickedness.
Yea, I shall walk through the valley of poverty and will
    fear no evil for thou, Heroin, art with me.
Thy Needle and Capsule comfort me.
Thou strippest the table of groceries in the presence of my
    family.
Thou robbest my head of reason.

101

My cup of sorrow runneth over.
Surely heroin addiction shall stalk me all the days of my
    life and I will dwell in the House of the Damned
    forever.[1]

This re-wording of the Twenty-third Psalm by a young heroin addict eloquently describes the utter hopelessness that comes from drug addiction. Along with financial ruin and physical deterioration, she describes her alienation from God. With this psalm was the following note:

Jail didn't cure me. Nor did hospitalization help me for
long. The doctor told my family it would have been better,
indeed kinder, if the person who got me hooked on dope
had taken a gun and blown my brains out. And I wish to
God he had. My God, how I wish it.[2]

Tragically this young woman committed suicide. She could find no way out of her addiction.

GETTING OUT OF ADDICTION

Despite the specter of failing health, loss of family or friends, time in prison, or an ultimate death, the drug user will continue on drugs. Eventually he or she will come to a state of hopelessness and despair. Paradoxically, this may actually be the best thing that ever happened to the abuser. Norman Miller, a staff member of Teen Challenge (a very effective Christian ministry for drug addicts), describes this as "the bottom falling out of the bottom." The drug user now has to look for answers to the dilemma outside of himself or herself.

In 1935 a stockbroker from the Midwest named Bill Wilson faced a similar dilemma with his alcoholism. He describes what he did when he reached bottom:

At the hospital I was separated from alcohol for the last
time. Treatment seemed wise, for I showed signs of delirium tremens.
    There I humbly offered myself to God, as I then under-
stood Him, to do with me as He would. I placed myself

unreservedly under His care and direction. I admitted for the first time that of myself I was nothing; that without Him I was lost. I ruthlessly faced my sins and became willing to have my new-found Friend take them away, root and branch. I have not had a drink since.[3]

Wilson became sober and went on to found Alcoholics Anonymous, which has helped millions to recover and also find a relationship with God (although not necessarily that kind of relationship associated with a religious experience).

To get free from addiction, the drug user has to commit his or her life to God and let him provide his healing power. In the authors' experience, this is the only solution that works (along with appropriate medical care, which is detailed in chapter 9). Our patients' changed lives attest to this. We are not talking about an instantaneous, miraculous cure. This does happen, but it is rare. Even if the withdrawal symptoms are miraculously removed, the road back to normal living is long and difficult. There is a process of spiritual recovery that all drug users must go through.

The "Twelve Steps" of Alcoholics Anonymous (AA) provide an excellent framework for this recovery. Regardless of the type of addiction, be it drugs, food, gambling, or something else, the twelve-step process works. Here are the twelve steps:

---

1. We admitted we were powerless over alcohol—that our lives had become unmanageable.
2. We came to believe that a Power greater than ourselves could restore us to sanity.
3. We made a decision to turn our will and our lives over to the care of God as we understood Him.
4. We made a searching and fearless moral inventory of ourselves.
5. We admitted to God, to ourselves, and to another human being, the exact nature of our wrongs.
6. We were entirely ready to have God remove all these defects of character.

(Continued)

7. We humbly asked Him to remove our shortcomings.

8. We made a list of all persons we had harmed, and became willing to make amends to them all.

9. We made direct amends to such people wherever possible, except when to do so would injure others.

10. We continued to take personal inventory and, when we were wrong, promptly admitted it.

11. We sought through prayer and meditation to improve our conscious contact with God as we understood Him, praying only for knowledge of His will for us and the power to carry that out.

12. Having had a spiritual awakening as the result of these steps, we tried to carry this message to alcoholics, and to practice these principles in all our affairs.

Even though the twelve steps are not overtly biblical, they provide a beautiful model for the process of change and growth. Despite this, many Christians are leery of using them or AA. Dr. Anderson Spickard, a committed Christian who is the medical director of Vanderbilt Institute for Treatment of Alcoholism, says this about the twelve-step process and AA:

Despite AA's unparalleled success with alcoholics, some Christians avoid participating in its program because of its seemingly vague spirituality and the use of phrases such as "Higher Power" and "God as you know Him." These people are convinced that the only bona fide recovery programs are those that name the name of Jesus, and when Jesus doesn't specifically get credit for the alcoholic's sobriety, they have trouble believing that the recovery is legitimate.

From my perspective as a physician, this view is shortsighted and prevents many people from getting the assistance they need. Alcoholics Anonymous has helped thousands of alcoholics from all religious persuasions, and Christian alcoholics have no trouble understanding the

"Higher Power" as the Lord Jesus. I have never known any alcoholic whose faith was damaged by the spiritual program of AA, but I know dozens of Christians who first committed themselves to Jesus Christ because of their contact with Christian AA members and because of the spiritual progress they made by following "The Twelve Steps." As one recovering alcoholic told me, "Alcoholics Anonymous won't get you to heaven, and it can't keep you out of hell, but it can keep you sober long enough to make up your own mind."[4]

The Steps to Recovery

We present a series of steps that each drug user must go through along the road to recovery from drug abuse. These steps are derived from the Twelve Steps of AA, and are biblically based. They include: *admitting hopelessness, committing your life to God, self-examination, letting God change you, being accountable and responsible, growing spiritually, and serving others.*

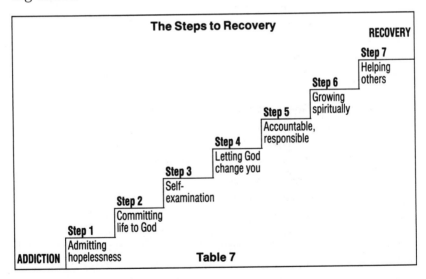

The Steps to Recovery

RECOVERY

Step 7 — Helping others

Step 6 — Growing spiritually

Step 5 — Accountable, responsible

Step 4 — Letting God change you

Step 3 — Self-examination

Step 2 — Committing life to God

Step 1 — Admitting hopelessness

ADDICTION

Table 7

STEP 1: *Admitting hopelessness.* (Step 1 of AA) The greatest problem facing the drug user is the unwillingness to admit: "I can't control the drug; the drug controls me." Drug abusers are powerless to do anything about their addiction. The classic answer, when asked about their drug problem, is: "I don't have a problem. I can quit whenever I want." Therefore, the road to recovery must start with the admission that the problem exists and that it is hopeless. The steps that led to drug addiction cannot be undone. Drug addicts cannot change themselves—they know that, because they have already quit a thousand times.

In Psalm 51:4 David tells God: "Against you, you only, have I sinned and done what is evil in your sight, so that you are proved right when you speak and justified when you judge." He was referring to his previous adultery with Bathsheba and murder of her husband. He acknowledged his wrongdoing and was willing to accept the consequences. He did not try to minimize the problems that he had created.

In Romans 7:19, 20, Paul admits this hopelessness: "For what I do is not the good I want to do; no, the evil I do not want to do—this I keep on doing. Now if I do what I do not want to do, it is no longer I who do it, but it is sin living in me that does it."

STEP 2: *Committing your life to God.* (Steps 2 and 3 of AA) Now that the hopelessness of addiction is acknowledged, answers need to be sought. God specializes in dealing with hopeless people and their problems. The drug user must be willing to give up control of his or her life and place it in God's hands.

Romans 5:8 shows the way out of this hopelessness: "But God demonstrates his own love for us in this: While we were still sinners, Christ died for us." When we commit our lives to Christ, we establish a personal relationship with him and he will begin to change our lives. In John 6:37 Jesus tells us: "All that the Father gives me will come to me, and whoever comes to me I will never drive away."

STEP 3: *Self-examination.* (Steps 4 and 5 of AA) It is very difficult and painful for people to admit that they have made mistakes, that they have hurt others. It may be even more difficult for substance abusers because of their strong feelings of guilt and shame. The issue here is not to increase the guilt level, but to effectively deal with it by confessing wrongs and allowing God to forgive us and remove the guilt.

The psalmist cries out in Psalm 139:23, 24: "Search me, O God, and know my heart; test me and know my anxious thoughts. See if there is any offensive way in me, and lead me in the way everlasting." 1 John 1:8, 9 describes the process: "If we claim to be without sin, we deceive ourselves and the truth is not in us. If we confess our sins, he is faithful and just and will forgive us our sins and purify us from all unrighteousness."

STEP 4: *Letting God change you.* (Steps 6 and 7 of AA) What we cannot do in our own power, God can do through his. Psalms 30:2 explains how this happens: "O Lord my God, I called to you for help and you healed me." Second Corinthians 5:17 offers great comfort and encouragement: "Therefore, if anyone is in Christ, he is a new creation; the old has gone, the new has come!" This process is lifelong. God is changing us from the inside out. The counselor can assure the converted drug user that he or she can become the kind of person that he or she always wanted to be, but could never be through one's own effort.

The ability to live drug-free comes from a change of attitude, change of friends, and a change of activities, and from living by the power of God's Holy Spirit. This has to be done one day at a time. Romans 12:2 puts it very eloquently: "Do not conform any longer to the pattern of this world, but be transformed by the renewing of your mind. . . ."

STEP 5: *Living responsibly and being accountable.* (Steps 8, 9 and 10 of AA) Irresponsibility and lack of accountability are hallmarks of a drug user's life. The excuse-making, conning, manipulating, lying, and stealing have to go. Relationships that have been harmed need to be repaired. If at all possible, wrongs need to be righted and forgiveness sought. For those not working, honest employment needs to be obtained. Though all of this is a tall order, when drug users begin to live responsibly, guilt will be lifted and they will feel much better about themselves. Relationships between family and friends will also begin to improve, enhancing the drug user's self-esteem.

Ephesians 4:25–32 beautifully details this new lifestyle:

Therefore each of you must put off falsehood and speak truthfully to his neighbor, for we are all members of one body. "In your anger do not sin." Do not let the sun go down while you are still angry, and do not give the devil a foothold. He who has been stealing must steal no longer, but must work, doing something useful with his own hands, that he may have something to share with those in need. Do not let any unwholesome talk come out of your mouths, but only what is helpful for building others up according to their needs, that it may benefit those who listen. And do not grieve the Holy Spirit of God, with whom you were sealed for the day of redemption. Get rid of all bitterness, rage and anger, brawling and slander, along with every form of malice. Be kind and compassionate to one another, forgiving each other, just as in Christ God forgave you.

STEP 6: *Growing spiritually.* (Step 11 of AA) In order to keep accomplishing these steps, the drug user must be continually growing spiritually. Spiritual growth has to start with an attitude of seeking God: "I love those who love me, and those who seek me find me" (Prov. 8:17). This is a wonderful and encouraging promise.

As the counselor knows, spiritual growth needs to include the areas of prayer, Bible study, worship, and relationships with other Christians. Prayer keeps the person in close touch with God; it is not just a time for giving him a shopping list, but is also a time for listening. What better model for prayer than Matthew 6:9–13:

"Our Father in heaven,
  hallowed be your name,
  your kingdom come,
  your will be done
  on earth as it is in heaven.
Give us today our daily bread.
Forgive us our debts,
  as we also have forgiven our debtors.
And lead us not into temptation,
  but deliver us from the evil one."

When the counselee studies God's Word, there is opportunity to learn about God himself, human nature, and one's self. As the person acknowledges and learns about self, then that person can allow God to make the changes that need to be made. Second Timothy 3:16 and 17 show how this works:

All scripture is God-breathed and is useful for teaching, rebuking, correcting and training in righteousness, so that the man of God may be thoroughly equipped for every good work.

Worship allows the counselee to show gratitude and thanks for what God is doing in his or her life. Psalm 100:4 tells us:

Enter his gates with thanksgiving
and his courts with praise;
give thanks to him and praise his name.

The counselor can emphasize that we cannot grow spiritually in a vacuum, but only in relationship with others who are also growing. This is not always easy for drug users, since they have lived very selfish and self-centered lives. Even though this may be threatening, it is absolutely essential if they are to maintain a drug-free state. Galatians 6:2 tells us that we need to:

Carry each other's burdens, and in this way you will fulfill the law of Christ.

STEP 7: *Helping others.* (Step 12 of AA) Spiritual growth is of little benefit unless the person takes what has been received from God (and learned in counseling) and uses it to help others. The counselor can encourage his or her client by pointing out that God's children find that the greatest pleasures in life come from meeting the needs of others. This pleasure is far greater than any drug can provide.

This principle is beautifully illustrated at the Last Supper. Jesus washed his disciples' feet, and then explained to them why he did so. He finished his discourse by telling them in

John 13:17: "Now that you know these things, you will be blessed [happy] if you do them." The ultimate purpose that God has for each person's life is that of serving others rather than himself. "Praise be to the God and Father of our Lord Jesus Christ, the Father of compassion and the God of all comfort, who comforts us in all our troubles, so that we can comfort those in any trouble with the comfort we ourselves have received from God" (2 Cor. 1:3, 4).

THE STORY OF A DRUG USER

The following is the true story of one person's battle with drugs.

Bruce was born into an upper middle-class family. He was only two years old when his parents were divorced. He lived with his mother and an older sister and brother. At age thirteen he tried pot for the first time. He recalls that it gave him a headache, but not much of a high. He used it several times a month, depending upon when his friends had it. His family knew nothing about his drug use. At the time he was doing okay in school, still participating in extracurricular activities, and still going to church.

At age fourteen he accepted Christ as Savior, but he continued to use pot once a week. His family still knew nothing about it because he would only do so away from home. His drug use progressed so that by age sixteen, he was using LSD, mescaline, and amphetamines, and drinking beer by the quart—this in addition to pot. He was also selling drugs to his friends to support his habit. Formerly an A and B student, he was now failing.

Things also got worse at home. Bruce was in constant conflict with his mother and would no longer help with any family responsibilities. His appearance grew disheveled. Finally, when he was asked to cut his hair he ran away. After three months he returned home, cut back his drug use and tried harder to get along at home. However, this did not last long. Bruce's drug use soon escalated to include tranquilizers and sleeping pills.

By age seventeen he had flunked out of school. His mother

could no longer tolerate his behavior. Bruce experienced mood swings between passivity and extreme anger, and lied constantly. He was never home and was totally undependable. He left home and moved to another city to live with a relative. In this new environment, his drug use decreased dramatically; he tried hard to cooperate, attending church again and reading his Bible, but the change was short-lived.

Now eighteen and working full-time, he found that drugs were even easier to come by in the new city, so his drug use escalated rapidly. He was smoking pot almost daily and shooting speed, and then taking Quaaludes to "come down." He lasted a little over a year in the relative's house. Always coming home late, not helping with expenses, and not cleaning up after himself, he was given an ultimatum—either live responsibly or move out. Bruce chose to move out. He was only nineteen, but he had already tried most every kind of illicit drug available.

For the next several years he moved from place to place, bounced from roommate to roommate. As soon as he wore out his welcome he moved on. His drug use continued as before— pot, alcohol, speed, tranquilizers, sleeping pills. He also discovered a new drug: cocaine. However, it was so expensive that he could rarely afford to use it.

Bruce also began college during this time. He had discovered that he liked working with computers and wanted to learn more, but he never made it to class on time and flunked out. His dreams and goals were going up in a puff of pot smoke.

By age twenty-one Bruce's drug-dealing caught up with him. He was arrested after selling tranquilizers to an undercover agent and was convicted, but placed on probation for seven years. Being arrested got his attention. He decided to settle down, to cut back his drug use, and to get married. While his new wife knew about his drug habit, he, ironically, did not know about hers. He soon discovered it and was devastated. The marriage was annulled after only six weeks.

Bruce was now very much alone. He became depressed, and slashed his wrists, and deliberately wrecked his car. He blamed his family, God, and everyone else for his problems—but not himself. His drug use remained unchanged—pot, booze, and pills. He was now working with computers and liked his job, so he also learned how to "control" his drug use in order to keep his job. He mastered the art of when to use drugs and when to stop and concerned himself with appearances, such as using eye drops to remove the redness.

By the time he reached age twenty-two Bruce had already lived a lifetime. The awareness of his pain and failure began to work on him. He became very much aware of the contrast between his life and that of his older brother. A Christian, his brother had always shown him love, despite his being hurt many times by Bruce's behavior. Furthermore, his brother kept confronting him about his drug use. Bruce drew closer to God. He started going to church again, reading his Bible and praying, and he cut down his pot use to once weekly. He was now just doing speed, sleeping pills, and booze on occasion.

At twenty-three he married for the second time, and he and his new wife moved back to his hometown. He had a new job in the computer field and life was getting better. However, he still maintained his drug use, ingesting pot, Quaaludes, and beer. With his new home, new job, and new marriage, he was very happy. He attended church regularly, but he was not growing spiritually. He and his wife would argue about his drug use, but he refused to give them up.

This second marriage lasted three years. One day his wife told him that she had never really loved him, and that she had only married him because she felt sorry for him. In reality they had never developed the closeness needed to make the marriage work. The main reason was the drugs.

Now that the bubble of happiness had burst, depression set in. He went back to drugs for solace, instead of to God. From occasional use, he increased his intake to an almost daily use of pot and Quaaludes, and he started using speed again and more alcohol. For the next two years, he stayed on the drug roller coaster, using enough to stay high, but controlling it to avoid losing his job. He went to church occasionally, but wasn't willing to let God have a part in his life. He didn't want to give up the drugs.

At age twenty-eight Bruce left his hometown for the second time and moved to another state, hoping that a change of environment would help him with his drug problem. It did. In the new city he had no drug connections and his drug use decreased dramatically. He was now using only pot and beer, and mainly on the weekends. At the same time he began going to church and studying the Bible more, but he did not want to get rid of the drugs. They were always there when he needed them, especially to blot out the stresses of work.

Bruce was getting established and enjoying his new location. He married for the third time and vowed that this time things would be different. He and his wife were going to follow God. Life was getting better, but then he met cocaine again. This new city was "cocaine city"; the drug was everywhere, used by many of his colleagues, and readily available. Bruce and his new wife used it together, and his use increased dramatically.

In order to come down from the cocaine high he drank, and his alcohol use also increased. Now the cost of drugs was getting out of hand. He and his wife never had any money despite their above average income. In order to pay for the increasing cost of his habit, Bruce started delivering cocaine to other users, acting as a middleman. He would get the cocaine from his connection, dilute it after taking the best part for himself, then deliver it. It seemed like the perfect setup—free cocaine.

Then marriage number three began to fall apart, for there was no center to it, except drugs. No amount of prayer, Bible reading, or church attendance would help. In fact, going to church was making things worse because guilt was beginning to build up. He felt very uncomfortable and hypocritical whenever he went. Bruce was now thirty.

In the next year, marriage number three ended. Now everything was in chaos again. Debts were piling up. New problems arose, including an arrest for driving while intoxicated and threats from a drug dealer he had cheated. His job, which had been an enjoyment, was now a nightmare, and it was soon lost. Now, everything was in ruins. He was bankrupt from the previous marriage; he had lost his home, his car, and most of his possessions. He quickly ran out of money and friends.

But one thing was different this time. Despite his drug use and all of its related problems, Bruce kept going to church. He knew that God wanted something better, something different for him. He was also receiving counseling from one of the pastors. Though his pastor-counselor did not condone the drug use, he did not reject him. Nor would he give him any money. But he did help with groceries and a place to stay. All the pieces were moving into place—God was not through with Bruce.

Out of work and out of money, but with time to kill, Bruce decided to visit his family. He wanted to look for a new job and change cities again, so he borrowed some money from his sister to finance the trip. Back in his hometown, he visited his mother. And while there he "borrowed" one of her credit cards. Before he left the city he went on a booze and cocaine binge, courtesy of the credit card.

He next went to visit his brother. Pretending to go to a friend's house, he had another night of booze and cocaine and didn't return until 4:00 A.M. His brother had suspected that Bruce was still having drug problems, and this episode confirmed it. He told Bruce to leave and decided that it was time to break off their relationship. He did not want to do anything to make it easier for Bruce to continue to use drugs.

Finally, Bruce had reached the end of the road. He had lost his best friend—his brother—and had alienated the rest of his family. He had no job and no hope for one, and was receiving threatening phone calls from people to whom he owed money. The bottom had fallen out of the bottom.

All of a sudden the "lights came on," and the drug-induced fog lifted. For the first time in his life Bruce realized that he was totally hopeless and helpless. Always in the past he had been somehow able to make things work out, to con and manipulate his way out of trouble—but not anymore. He knew that God had been patient with him. He also knew that if things didn't change, either death or prison was lurking around the corner.

Bruce decided to let God have complete control of his life. He can't completely explain what happened, but says that he knew that he had to get serious with God. There was no other choice. He and God had to do business just between the two of them.

Bruce gave up the drugs, and things began to change dramatically. His counselor at church wanted to have him hospitalized, but that fell through at the last minute. However, by God's grace and through participation in an outpatient treatment program, Bruce was able to stay clean on his own. He hadn't been drug-free since he was a teenager.

He began to grow spiritually, moreso in just a few months than in all the years since he had accepted Christ as a teenager. He found that he really enjoyed his life of being drug-free, and his new walk with God gave him a happiness he had never known while on drugs.

Now that he was clean both mentally and spiritually, God began to work in a wonderful way. Bruce applied for a new job in another city. He was one of one hundred applicants for this job. He told his prospective employer about the past and they still hired him! Later that year he married again, this time drug-free and to a woman who was committed to put God first in her life.

Today Bruce is growing spiritually, living responsibly, and rebuilding relationships destroyed during the drug years. He is now an asset to his church and community, rather than a liability. He has set new goals for himself, including learning how to handle money, controlling anger, developing personal relationships, showing more love for his spouse, and restoring his physical fitness. He wants to help others who have drug problems to find God's love.

As this is being written, Bruce is now thirty-three, and in his second year of drug-free living. He has never been happier in his life, a happiness that drugs could never provide. He is also very aware that he has to live life one day at a time, for he still feels the pull of cocaine and alcohol. However, he knows that by God's grace and power he will be able to stay drug-free.

WHAT ABOUT THOSE WHO DON'T WANT HELP?

Each individual must make his or her choice to accept or reject God's healing power. We who are concerned cannot do it for the person. It is hard to stand by and watch our loved ones wallow in drug abuse and reject God's healing power (if they so choose). One ray of hope is that the drug user knows deep inside that help is needed, and this may lead the individual to turn to God and seek professional help.

What approach should you take when your counselee or a relative resists giving up drugs? (Chapter 5 lists several steps.) The most important thing is to *never* stop praying for the one who is addicted. This is not easy; it takes time and much effort. And it will require an attitude of forgiveness on your part, especially if you have been repeatedly hurt and disappointed. Don't retaliate, but be willing to wait. The time you spend in prayer can change *your* attitudes and behavior. This will make you more effective in dealing with the abuser.

PRACTICAL ADVICE FOR THE RECOVERING DRUG USER

The following guidelines could be shared with the drug user who wants to change:

- The time to become drug-free is today. Drug-free means to be free of *all* drugs, even alcohol. This is impossible to do on one's own. You need to participate in a legitimate program of recovery.
- Recovery from drug addiction is a lifelong process and not just a one-time event. You must "work" your program in a step-by-step process. It will take time for your mind and body to heal and also time for God to change you.
- Get help from someone qualified. You shouldn't try to do it on your own.
- Don't give up if you should relapse. It is never too late to get back on the right track. God is the God of the second chance, and more.
- Don't struggle with drugs in your own strength. We must depend upon God's strength and power to stay drug-free. Read Galatians 5:16 and Philippians 4:13.
- You must stay away from all drugs (including alcohol) and drug-using friends. To associate with them is one of the easiest ways to relapse. As 1 Corinthians 15:33 states: "Do not be misled: 'Bad company corrupts good character.'"
- Don't be surprised when you are tempted to use drugs again. Temptation in itself is not sinful—it is what you do with it that matters. (See 1 Corinthians 10:13, James 1:13–15.)

- Recognize that it is easier to lie to yourself than to anyone else you know. You must be aware of your ability to rationalize wrong attitudes and wrong behavior. (See Jeremiah 17:9, Psalm 51:6.)
- Don't become proud and self-sufficient once you become drug-free, as you cannot claim credit for your recovery. "Pride goes before destruction, and a haughty spirit before a fall" (Prov. 16:18).
- Have confidence in God. He has your best interest at heart. Murphy's Law does not control the life of the Christian. (See Romans 8:28.)
- Walk with God one day at a time. He knows your problems and your needs. (See Matthew 6:25–34, Philippians 4:6,7.)
- Take time to pray every day. Prayer is the "glue" that keeps us close to God. It is through prayer that God changes us. (Read James 5:13–18.)
- Read your Bible every day. God's Word has the answers for your problems and the direction you need. (Memorize Proverbs 3:5, 6.)
- Attend church weekly. This is where you can worship and serve God. You will grow when you give of yourself to others. (Read Hebrews 10:24, 25.)
- Maintain a "support" system, a group of other Christians with whom you can share your struggles and receive encouragement. This will help you cope with the pressures of life. (Note Galatians 6:1, 2.)
- Memorize the following prayer:

The Serenity Prayer

God, grant me the Serenity
to accept the things I cannot change,
Courage to change the things I can,
and Wisdom to know the difference.

CHAPTER EIGHT

PICKING UP THE PIECES

HOW TO DEAL WITH THE ANGER AND HURT IN THE ADDICT'S FAMILY

A Question of Control

In the still of the night
My only son cries out—"I am on drugs"
On my heart that word tugs.

My mind says, "No, this cannot be true,
I did the best I could for you;
Have lived my life for you,"

I feel fear, shame, desperation, isolation
Anger well inside my soul:

"Lord, why me," I cry,
"For I am in control."

The search for help begins
It is you, not I, I must mend,
Deep in denial, my cry remains
"Not my child, Lord, not I to blame."

Reality intervenes—"Am I to blame, or
Is codependency my disease?
When I give up the need to control
Will I find peace within my soul?"

Reality is painful, but true
Joy replaces the anger in my soul
God reveals my goal:
To love you and let you go
For it is He who is in control.

—*Vivian Brooks*

This heart-rending poem eloquently expresses the grief and anguish that comes from losing a loved one to substance abuse. More often than not the loss does not involve actual death, but it is just as painful. We can accept death, disease, or desertion much easier when it is due to some other cause. However, some unknown element makes the loss seem more tragic when substance abuse is involved.

CODEPENDENCY

In chapter 6 we highlighted the effects of substance abuse upon the nonaddicted family members. The relationship and the interaction that take place between the substance abuser and the family is called *codependency.*[1] No family member remains untouched—all are affected. Unfortunately, many family members deny their anger, hurt, and resentment. However, these damaged emotions are like a rattlesnake lying in a field— all is apparently peaceful, but when the snake is disturbed, it strikes with venomous fury.

Although the concept of codependency first originated to describe the pathology within the chemically dependent family, it

is now recognized as resulting from involvement in any dysfunctional family. Other dysfunctional family systems include:
1. the emotionally or psychologically disturbed family system,
2. the physically, sexually abusive family system, or
3. the fundamentalistic or rigidly dogmatic family system.[2]

The main problem related to codependency is that once the substance abuser enters treatment and becomes drug-free the family members believe that their problems are over. In many ways, they have just begun. It is all too common that when the abuser gets better, the family gets worse. The emotional damage that they have suffered because of substance abuse has not been dealt with. This is why it is imperative that the entire family go through the treatment process along with the abuser. They must go through the process and not around it.

This emotional damage results in three major areas of loss in the lives of a substance abuser's family members. This applies whether they are the spouse, the child, the parent, or even a close friend. The sense of loss along with grief, anger, and resentment leads to the conflict. These losses are three: *the loss of a loved one, the loss of trust, and the loss of normalcy.*

Loss of a Loved One

When one loses a loved one to a life of substance abuse, the feeling of loss is as great as if that person had actually died. (Unfortunately, death does take place all too often.) In some ways this loss is greater than that of death because the drug user is an ever-present reminder, a source of continued pain and sorrow. This is especially true if the person is still living in the household.

Many questions arise in the minds of the drug user's family. They ask, did I cause them to drink or use drugs? What could I have done differently? Will they ever be drug-free? Will they ever be normal again? What did I do wrong? Along with these questions the family has a great sense of guilt and responsibility which is frequently made worse as the substance abuser blames others for the addiction and its resultant problems.

Ultimately, this loss of a loved one leads to grief, the same kind of grief one experiences when dealing with death. There

COUNSELING FOR SUBSTANCE ABUSE AND ADDICTION ————

is, normally, a series of stages through which one passes in grief. They are denial, anger, bargaining, depression, and acceptance.[3] By working through each stage, one can have victory instead of defeat.

Denial. Denial is a mechanism that allows one to avoid dealing with a very painful situation. Unfortunately, if the loss of a loved one due to substance abuse is denied, then no one can get well, neither the abuser nor especially the family. The first step to solving a problem is admitting—however painful that may be—that the problem exists and help is needed.

Anger. Once the reality of the loss sinks in, then anger takes over. Usually this anger is directed toward the abuser, toward other family members, and also toward God. It is important that this anger be recognized and acknowledged, and not repressed.

Many Christians have the impression that they should not get angry, but even Jesus got angry when there was injustice. Instead of stifling anger, it needs to be dealt with consciously. But how? First, one must go to God and acknowledge the anger, and then ask for the ability to forgive and forget. Second, the energy released by the anger should be channeled into changing oneself for the better.

Bargaining. As the anger subsides, a strange kind of hope arises. The thought is *maybe I can bargain with God and/or the abuser to change the situation.* It is a last-ditch effort to exert control, to change the outcome in one's favor. At this point, the family contends with a profusion of begging, pleading, and scheming—anything rather than having to face the pain of the situation.

Depression. After bargaining fails, the awareness hits home that the loss is inevitable and unchangeable. Now depression sets in. Things are hopeless. Self-pity reigns. All life is drudgery. "Why go on living?" one is tempted to ask. Another common feeling is, "this is hopeless, nothing can be done about it." Unfortunately, this stage frequently lasts the longest and delays many families from getting help.

Acceptance. Fortunately, at this stage hope is on the horizon. Once a problem is accepted as existing, then solutions can be sought. However, the solutions don't work like magic nor are they easy. They must come from God and with the help of knowledgeable and properly trained individuals. As Proverbs 3:5, 6 tells us, "Trust in the Lord with all your heart and lean not on your own understanding; in all your ways acknowledge him, and he will make your paths straight."

In helping people with acceptance, we need to remember some "can'ts" and some "cans."

We *can't* change anybody but ourselves.
We *can't* change the past.
We *can't* always get our own way.
We *can't* always make people do what we want them to do.

We *can* change ourselves.
We *can* change our future.
We *can* change how we feel when we don't get our way.
We *can* change how we act when people don't do what we want them to do.[4]

When one is hurting due to the addiction of a loved one, how does that person let God provide the solution to the hurt? The following true story, related by Philip Yancey in his book *Where Is God When It Hurts?* beautifully illustrates both the agony of loss and the provision from God.[5]

Christian Reger [a German pastor imprisoned at Dachau for resisting Hitler] will tell the horror stories if you ask. But he will never stop there. He goes on to share his faith—how at Dachau, he was visited by a God who loves.

"Nietzsche said a man can undergo torture if he knows the why of his life," Reger told me. "But I, here at Dachau, learned something far greater. I learned to know the Who of my life. He was enough to sustain me then, and is enough to sustain me still."

It was not always so. After his first month in Dachau, Reger had, like Elie Wiesel, abandoned all hope in a loving God. The odds against His existence, from the perspective of a Nazi prisoner, were just too great. Then, in July, 1941, something happened to challenge his doubt.

Prisoners were allowed only one letter a month, and exactly one month from the date of his incarceration, Christian Reger received the first news from his wife. The letter, carefully clipped in pieces by censors, chatted about the family and her love for him. At the bottom was printed a reference to Bible verses: Acts 4:26–29. Reger looked up the verses, part of a speech by Peter and John after being released from prison.

"'The kings of the earth take their stand and the rulers gather together against the Lord and against his anointed One.' Indeed Herod and Pontius Pilate met together with the Gentiles and the people of Israel in this city to conspire against your holy servant Jesus, whom you anointed. They did what your power and will had decided beforehand should happen. Now, Lord, consider their threats and enable your servants to speak your work with boldness" (NIV).

That afternoon Reger was to face interrogators, the most frightening experience in the camp. He would be called on to name fellow Christians, and if he gave in to pressures, those Christians would be captured and possibly killed. There was a good chance he would be beaten with clubs or tortured with electricity if he refused to cooperate with the interrogation. The verses meant little to him. What possible help could God be at a time like this?

Reger moved to the waiting area outside the interrogation room. He was trembling. The door opened, and a fellow minister whom Reger had never met came out. Without looking at Reger or changing the expression on his face, he walked to him, slipped something into Reger's coat pocket, and walked away. Seconds later SS guards appeared and ushered Reger inside the room. The interrogations went well; they were surprisingly easy and involved no violence.

When Reger arrived back at the barracks, he was sweating from tension. He breathed deeply for several moments, trying to calm himself, then crawled into his bunk, covered with straw. Suddenly he remembered the strange incident with the other minister. He reached in his pocket and pulled out a matchbox. Oh, he thought, what a kind gesture. Matches are a priceless commodity in the barracks. Inside, however, there were no matches, just a folded slip of paper. Reger unfolded the paper, and his heart pounded hard against his chest. Neatly printed on the paper was this reference: Acts 4:26–29.

It was a miracle, a message from God. There was no way that minister could have seen his letter from his wife—he did not even know the minister. God had arranged the event as a demonstration that He was still alive, still able to strengthen, still worthy of trust.

Christian Reger was transformed from that moment. It was a small miracle, as miracles go, but it was enough to found his faith in bedrock that could not be jarred by the atrocities, murders, and human injustice he would see the next four years in Dachau.

"God did not rescue me and make my suffering easier. He simply proved to me that He was still alive, and He still knew I was here."

Loss of Trust

When one lives with a substance abuser one learns very quickly not to trust that person. Substance abusers are not trustworthy. There are millions of broken promises, lies, excuses, and rationalizations. Not trusting the abuser may be both necessary and protective while the abuser is actually addicted, but it is harmful and counterproductive when he or she is trying to sober up and stay clean.

If you have had little experience with drug users, you may ask, why don't the family members rejoice at the sobriety and be supportive? The answer lies in the fact that once trust is lost, it is not easily restored. Furthermore, it can't be restored until the emotions damaged by the substance abuse within the family are repaired. The major emotion behind this loss of trust is *anger*.

One of the best examples of this anger is that of the older brother in Luke's (15:11–32) story of the Prodigal Son. Instead of being glad that his brother had returned and repented from his riotous living, he was angry that he was being shown love. Dr. Vernon Johnson comments on this anger and how it is the same kind of anger that affects the alcoholic and his family:

> Obviously, this [the prodigal brother's anger] describes many emotions of the family or other meaningful people around the alcoholic. Their spiritual and emotional distress is precisely the same, the only difference being the degree. The spouse daily bears the burden of the alcoholic's progressive defection from responsibility. He or she has to take over both roles: mother and father. Eventually, the spouse may become both planner and provider. This is done conscientiously and consistently. The spouse bears the responsibility for decision-making and keeps things together somehow. And the alcoholic projects self-loathing upon the spouse, who is frequently verbally abused and insulted for this very selflessness.
>
> The spouse tries to shield their problems from the rest of the community, covering up for the alcoholic in every possible way. This may involve lying to employers and relatives and neighbors, all at great cost to self-esteem. The spouse comes to believe finally that, while others may live and enjoy life in normal ways, it is necessary to live for others, and that somewhere—somehow—there must be adequate reward for such sacrifice. [This applies whether the spouse is either wife or husband.]
>
> And then, after all this, the alcoholic goes to the hospital and the spouse is told that the husband or wife is coming back well again, ready to start life over and capable of doing it! Quite apart from all the other concerns—not the least of which are the spouse's own basic personal inadequacy and fears that this may be just another false hope— the spouse is now told he or she is to overlook the past and forget it. It's too much! Forgive, after all the suffering that's been caused—impossible!
>
> Forgiveness is costly, and these costs are too often minimized, or forgiveness itself is confused with repression. "I'll forgive you, but I can never forget it," or "I'll try to forget

it, but I'll never be able to forgive you," are statements which ignore the basic elements required in forgiveness.[6]

How is the anger dealt with? First, the family members must recognize and accept the fact that they are indeed angry. Second, they need to understand the appropriateness of anger (it is okay to be angry). Third, they need to learn how to process and work through their anger (this includes how to express anger appropriately). Fourth, they need to learn how to forgive despite the pain and difficulty.

Concerning forgiveness, Jesus made it very clear in the Gospels that forgiveness is essential, not optional. We need to forgive because God has forgiven us (Eph. 4:32). We need to forgive because God can't forgive us until we forgive others (Matt. 6:14, 15). Finally, we need to forgive so that we don't torment ourselves (Matt. 18:34, 35).

These specific steps will allow you as counselor to facilitate the forgiveness needed in the healing process and in dealing with this anger. "Psychologist Raymond Novaco tells us that anger and resentments are incited, maintained, and inflamed by 'self-talk,' the things we say and think to ourselves. We dwell on injustices and resentments, letting them smolder on for hours, days, weeks, months, even years after the initial provocation has passed. We may live in the present, but our emotions are stuck in the superglue of the past. We often don't recognize our own 'stinking thinking.'"[7]

When your counselees start to feel angry, suggest that they ask themselves the following questions:[8]

1. What am I feeling?
2. Why am I feeling this way?
3. What can I do about it?
4. What am I going to do about it?

These questions revolve around the letter *I*. When anger appears, individuals need to face the responsibility (the *I*) for initiating it, rather than blame something or someone else for causing it. The *I* of anger usually comes because the person feels that "I am being mistreated," "I don't deserve this," "I'm not getting what I want or need." We will want to help such persons see that they may not be able to change the situation which provokes the anger, but they are responsible for how they respond to it.

Just as there are four questions to ask concerning why people are angry, there are also four steps to take in dealing with anger:

1. Know why your anger develops.
2. Deal with your "stinking thinking."
3. Take responsibility for your thoughts, feelings, and actions.
4. Learn how to appropriately handle and express anger.

There are two practical points to remember in a person's learning how to control anger. First, he or she needs to talk to someone else about the anger. This someone else includes both God and another person who knows how to listen. Psalm 91:15 tells us:

> He will call upon me, and I will answer him;
> I will be with him in trouble, . . .

The Psalms are full of expressions of anger and anguish, but they are also full of the answers for the hurting soul.

Second, the person needs to deal with anger when it arises. If the individual does not, it only smolders and grows; finally, when the anger is dealt with, the problems it has created are much greater than they would have been if handled earlier. Ephesians 4:26 (NASB) tells us: "Be angry, and yet do not sin; do not let the sun go down on your anger. . . ." If anger is dealt with constructively, it does not have to lead to destructive consequences.

Loss of Normalcy

John is a faithful member of his church. He attends and participates in all church activities. One day, he comes to his pastor in tears saying he doesn't understand what is happening to him. He feels suicidal. He is having trouble with his relationships at home. He feels he is failing the Lord.

At first his pastor thought that John was having either an episode of depression or else a midlife crisis. After careful questioning, he discovered that John's father was an alcoholic. John had no idea how his father's addiction was affecting him now as an adult. "I'm a Christian and I've never even tasted alcohol," he says in anguish.

John's loss of normalcy as a child is very likely the source of his depression. As we discussed in chapter 6, the turmoil and unpredictability caused by substance-abusing parents leave scars which are carried into adulthood. Substance-abusing families demonstrate similar attitudes or coping mechanisms which are handed down from parent to child. The primary "don'ts" of the child of alcoholics as described by Claudia Black, a leader in the field, are: *"don't talk," "don't trust,"* and *"don't feel."*[9] While these attitudes may make it easier to survive during childhood, they are counterproductive in adulthood.

"The notion of the 'child within' has been one of the most helpful concepts for adult children of alcoholics," says Sharon Wegscheider-Cruse, a leader in the treatment of adult children of alcoholics. "We have seen how children of alcoholics have been encouraged to grow up fast, to become small versions of adulthood. . . . The time has come, now that we understand this phenomenon, to go back inside and retrieve the little lost child who has been waiting to grow up and have its proper place in our lives."[10]

How does this "lost child" grow up? First, codependent family members will have to go through the grief process presented earlier in this chapter. Second, they will have to go through a simultaneous healing process, which involves the following steps or goals:[11]

1. *Letting down the defenses.* If one is to recover from the emotional damage of his or her childhood, the defenses (the roles outlined in chapter 6) that developed at that time need to be acknowledged and dealt with. Continuing with them will only insure failure as an adult. Being in a group (Al-Anon, Adult Children of Alcoholics) will allow such people to be

themselves, open, and honest in a nonthreatening environment. Although doing this is scary, it is essential for the healthy emotional growth of these people, so they will not repeat the mistakes of the parent(s).

2. *Dealing with negative emotions.* As defenses are let down, many negative emotions surface:

rage	hurt	discomfort
concern	embarrassment	resentment
tension	jealousy	sadness
anger	shame	guilt

These may come in a torrent, but they need to come out. It is important not to feel guilty for having them and it is also most important not to dwell on them. These emotions are a product of a childhood in a "sick" family. You as a counselor must help the individual accept these emotions and not feel guilty for having them.

3. *Learning to think, feel, live in a healthy way.* When something that is harmful is removed, it must be replaced with something good or beneficial. We are not suggesting a "Pollyanna" approach to life—that is, denying the unpleasant. Rather, we are talking about living life in a healthy and positive way, and finding enjoyment in healthy activities and relationships.

This may be best summed up in the words of Jesus in John 10:10 (NASB): "The thief comes only to steal, and kill, and destroy; I came that they might have life, and might have it abundantly." The "thief," for some people, seems to be drugs and alcohol. "Abundance" here does not refer to material possessions, but quality of life. God wants the drug abusers and their family members to be all that they were created to be.

4. *Acknowledging one's codependency.* Children growing up in an "addicted family" are going to be affected by it. Through no fault of their own they became part of a cycle of codependency. Through denial, distorted thinking, and compulsive behavior, the family experiences functional impairment, bringing on a sense of helplessness. This feeling fosters shame and inadequacy giving rise to anger, which surfaces as guilt and resentment. As the anger continues and is internalized, depression and

a feeling of hopelessness develop and addictive behavior is adopted as a way of coping. The illustration that follows illustrates this cycle.

Breaking out of this cycle is imperative. It is vital for the counselor to question all clients (regardless of their presenting problem) about possible substance abuse in the family. It is frequently the "family secret"; but the cycle of codependent behavior will repeat itself unless it is broken.

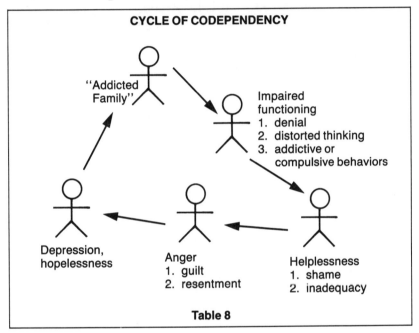

CYCLE OF CODEPENDENCY

"Addicted Family"

Impaired functioning
1. denial
2. distorted thinking
3. addictive or compulsive behaviors

Depression, hopelessness

Anger
1. guilt
2. resentment

Helplessness
1. shame
2. inadequacy

Table 8

5. *Making a commitment to a recovery program or support group.* The adult child of the alcoholic or drug user will always feel and know that he or she is different from those who grew up in healthy families. Despite the fact that the emotional damage has been repaired, scars remain just as they do on our skin when it is injured. By participating in a support group, the adult child can receive the support and comfort from others who have known similar sorrow.

Lord, make me a channel of thy peace—that where there is hatred, I may bring love—that where there is wrong, I may bring the spirit of forgiveness—that where there is error, I may bring truth—that where there is doubt, I may bring faith—that where there is despair, I may bring hope—that where there are shadows, I may bring joy. Lord, grant that I may seek rather to comfort than to be comforted—to understand, than to be understood—to love, than to be loved. For it is by self-forgetting that one finds. It is by forgiving that one is forgiven. It is by dying that one awakens to Eternal Life. Amen.

St. Francis of Assisi

CHAPTER NINE

WHAT REALLY WORKS IN TREATMENT

A LOOK AT INPATIENT, OUTPATIENT, AND RESIDENTIAL PROGRAMS

Dear Herlinda, Naomi, Hector, Frank, and Doctors,

I just had to write and tell you how I feel about you all and the TOUCH program. I was going to come by and tell you in person, however, I always choke up and forget all I really want to say. You all are great people and I love you all for being such good friends—for all the support and unconditional love you gave us.

As you all know we have gone to MHMR [state-operated drug treatment program]. I wanted to tell you all before leaving, but I felt so guilty about letting you down. I know that I am the one that lost out because I am still not drug-free but I just was not ready. Even though I prayed to God to give me strength to get through, I kept getting that feeling gnawing at me to fix. And it kept getting stronger as my dose [of methadone] got weaker. Maybe it was because I did not have enough faith in the Lord and did not trust totally in Him. But I did truly try to do all of this. Anyway I just wasn't strong enough and I am sure this is better than fixing again.

Those of you that have been through all this know that it does not come easy. I just know that it is disappointing to you all there at TOUCH, who work so hard for us, who devote so much of your time to us—to see us drug-free and good Christians, living a good Christian life. That is why I wanted to write and tell you all that even though we are not drug-free you did not waste your efforts totally.

We left TOUCH with a lot more than what we came in with. My whole family found the Lord, accepting Him as their personal Savior. You all showed us how to pray and read the Bible (daily), how to praise the Lord in song and in fellowship and attending Bible study and church on Sunday. All of this would probably never have happened.[1]

The above letter was sent to the staff of the TOUCH Drug Rehabilitation Program by a couple who spent many months in treatment. TOUCH stands for Transforming Others Under Christ's Hand and is a Christ-centered outpatient treatment program (in San Antonio, Texas) that works mainly with heroin addicts.

This letter shows the beautiful changes that can take place during the treatment of addiction. It also is a sobering reminder that the road to being drug-free is long and difficult. There are no quick cures, no easy answers.

Though this man and woman tried very hard, they did not feel ready to quit methadone detoxification for their heroin addiction. This does not necessarily mean that they were spiritually weak. It points out that each individual changes and grows at a different rate. Change may take place more slowly in an outpatient treatment program, and may be less dramatic than that seen in an inpatient program.

"I treat, but God heals," said the father of modern American medicine, William Osler. This is what effective treatment is all about. As we have shown in earlier chapters, drug addiction is both a medical disease and a spiritual illness. We have also presented the steps necessary for spiritual recovery. The rest of this chapter will highlight the medical aspects of treatment.

Christians should not despair if they cannot find a Christian-oriented treatment program in their area. God works through individuals, both Christian and non-Christian, to accomplish his purposes. The medical treatment is just the beginning of recovery from addiction. Once a person is sober-minded, then he or she can more clearly hear the voice of God.

GETTING THE DRUG USER INTO TREATMENT

The first step in treating drug addiction is actually getting the drug user to agree to treatment. This is also the most difficult. As we mentioned in chapter 5, denial perpetuates drug addiction. Until some form of crisis enters the addict's life, he or she will usually not seek treatment. This crisis will frequently present itself in one of the following areas:

Legal. Many drug addicts will have to steal, sell drugs, or even prostitute themselves in order to support their habit. They also get arrested for driving under the influence, for possession of drugs, or for unruly behavior. Eventually, the drug user will get caught in illegal activities. Many courts are now mandating treatment in place of going to jail or prison.

Family. The spouse will frequently leave the drug user because of the effects of the person's behavior upon the family. This is a crisis for the addict because this may be the only emotional support the person has. This makes him or her more open for treatment.

Medical. As their health deteriorates, addicts realize that their drug use is killing them. They may be aware that their behavior is out of control, or it may take a life-threatening problem such as violent injury (shooting, stabbing, car wreck), overdose, or a serious health problem.

Work. Drug addicts are poor employees due to their absenteeism and erratic performance. They will eventually be threatened with the loss of their jobs or actually be fired. Many employers are mandating treatment as a condition of continued employment.

Intervention. Substance abusers are given the option of receiving treatment as a part of a planned confrontation and intervention. The intervention process is detailed in chapter 5.

CHOOSING THE RIGHT TYPE OF PROGRAM

Once the decision for treatment is made, the next step is to decide what type of program is best suited for the drug user. Generally, outpatient treatment is less expensive and less disruptive to one's work and family responsibilities. Outpatient treatment works best for those who are in good health and who have a strong desire to become drug-free.

Inpatient treatment has the advantage of being intensive and removing the drug user from both the drug and the drug-using environment. Those who are in poor health from their addiction and whose living environment is negatively affected by other factors usually need an inpatient program.

Residential programs are designed to offer a long-term (usually six months or more) controlled environment in which the recovering drug user can learn how to live without drugs. This requires a very structured program which keeps the patient constructively busy and away from drugs and drug-using friends. This type of program is best for the adolescent or young adult who is motivated to stop taking drugs, does not need hospitalization, and who needs an external support system.

Other considerations include one's financial resources, health insurance coverage, kinds of programs available, the type of drugs being used, medical complications, and the type of available aftercare. In making a decision encourage your counselees to receive recommendations from a physician, or from the local medical society, those who have used a particular program in which you are interested, and parent or family support groups.

TREATMENT MODALITIES

Outpatient Therapy

An outpatient program will typically provide medical detoxification (if needed), weekly meetings, individual and group counseling, peer counseling, and frequent urine drug screening. The latter two are probably the most important in helping the drug user stay clean. The addict can't con other addicts—they will confront the person about attitudes or behaviors that could lead to relapse. The urine drug screen is a necessary deterrent, as it helps the drug user say no to temptation.

Inpatient Treatment

The typical inpatient treatment program is much more intensive. It usually includes medical detoxification, patient education, group and individual therapy, family involvement and counseling, occupational therapy, recreational therapy, social services, introduction to a group such as Al-Anon, or Nar-Anon, and preparation for aftercare.

Residential Programs

A residential program may best be described as a "habilitation" rather than a rehabilitation program. This is due to the fact that many drug users have never finished going through the normal emotional, intellectual, and spiritual growth process. They need to "grow up."

A residential program will usually offer dormitory-style living, daily chores, family-style meals, and a fairly disciplined environment. Additionally, there may be educational and vocational training, group activities, and participation in the maintenance of the facility. Appendix 3 lists several excellent residential programs.

WHEN IS HOSPITALIZATION NECESSARY?

Here are some general guidelines for deciding when hospitalization is required. It is advisable when:

- One is highly addicted and needs medical detoxification. This is usually required for alcohol, barbiturate, and multiple-drug users. It is sometimes necessary for persons using cocaine or heroin, and those addicted to prescription drugs.
- The user is threatening to harm himself/herself, or another family member.
- Addict's health is deteriorating. Especially important for alcoholics.
- Addict cannot care for self, or has no family support at home.
- Addict is living with another active drug user.
- Addict is unwilling to attend an outpatient program.
- Addict has relapsed despite previous outpatient treatment.

Criteria for Selection of a Treatment Program

Quality varies greatly among treatment programs; some are excellent while others are very poor. A treatment program may look good on the surface, but that does not mean that it is effective and worthwhile. You as counselor will need to get recommendations from those who are familiar with or have used the particular program that you are considering recommending. The following criteria represent the essential elements to be found in the best programs.

1. *A blend of the spiritual and disease concepts of substance abuse.* The best programs appreciate that substance abuse is a spiritual as well as a medical sickness. The process often begins with "innocent" choices to dabble in unwise, risky, and even sinful practices. The principles of scriptural living, once violated, soon allow the person to sink slowly but steadily into the quicksand of more extensive drug or alcohol use. As the person sinks in deeper, like someone caught in quicksand, there is no longer an option of free choice; the only way is down, and down deeper still. The drug addict can no more simply choose to stop using a drug without help than a person chest deep in quicksand can choose to stop sinking and walk out of the sand. Both are trapped and both will die without

outside help. The addict must have effective treatment if he or she is to escape the inevitable downward pull of the disease which has now taken over.

2. *A commitment to a drug-free environment and a goal of total abstinence.* Effective drug and alcohol rehabilitation programs believe that substance abuse is a chronic, noncurable disease. This means that abstinence from all mind-altering drugs is necessary for one to become drug-free and live in a true state of recovery. Also, in order for substance abusers to deal rationally with their emotional and behavioral problems, they need to be free of the influence of mind-altering drugs. It is essential to place them in an environment that is drug and alcohol free. This means that visitors are restricted and that patients are carefully monitored to prevent drug usage while in treatment.

3. *A strong personal spiritual emphasis.* While it is up to the professional team to treat the substance abuser with the utmost of their skills, it is God who is the ultimate healer of the whole person. Unless the spiritual bankruptcy of the substance abuser is addressed and his or her relationship with God revitalized, then the likelihood of a successful and long-lasting recovery is slim. Recovering from an addiction is hard work. The apostle Paul knew where the real power for change in an individual's life has its origin. "For it is God who is at work in you, both to will and to work for His good pleasure" (Phil. 2:13 NASB).

4. *Competent medical and nursing care.* The disease of addiction to drugs or alcohol is a serious one, and expert medical care is often needed to stabilize the recovering addict physically. Dietary counseling is essential here as well, as substance abusers are often malnourished.

5. *Education about the disease process of drug addiction and the effects of the drugs themselves.* The good programs work at making sure the recovering substance abuser understands how addiction starts, what are its stages, the effects of the drugs, and how the "mind games" of the addict serve to perpetuate the addiction process. The means of denial and manipulation, the masks of deception, and influence of family

pressures should be exposed and explained to the recovering addict over and over again.

6. *Goal-setting and nonchemical coping skills.* The substance abuser has often lost the ability to set, work toward, and attain reasonable goals. He or she "solves" problems by turning to a chemical of abuse. Good programs work diligently at helping the recovering addict deal with life goals, using new coping techniques that don't involve chemical usage.

7. *Group therapy, interpersonal support, and peer accountability.* Recovery is hard and frequently painful work. The emotional cost is high and the recovering addict will need the *daily* work of high-quality group therapy while in the inpatient program. (Group therapy in outpatient programs can be less frequent.) Such therapy often helps addicts see themselves with the psychological camouflage stripped away. Becoming accountable to other recovering addicts without any easy escape will bring both the truth and the lies to the surface of one's personality, thus allowing the work of honest recovery to proceed.

8. *Family therapy, family activities, and communication skills.* Substance abuse is one of the great destroyers of the family unit. Substance abuse is to a family what termites are to a house, slowly eating it away until the structure collapses. For this reason, a good program will make a great effort to involve the addict's family in a variety of therapeutic activities, including: family and marital counseling, communication exercises, and activities together with the family both in and out of the hospital, to rebuild unity, intimacy, and trust.

9. *Participation in Alcoholics Anonymous (AA), Narcotics Anonymous (NA), Cocaine Anonymous (CA), Al-Anon, Nar-Anon, and Al-Ateen.* The better programs recognize the long-standing proven worth of these self-help programs and will provide opportunities for their patients to participate in them regularly while in treatment at their facility.

We understand the difficulty that some people have with AA. However, the twelve-step approach has been the most effective one for the past fifty years. It is also widely used in most other kinds of addiction, including addiction to food, sex, and gambling. Despite the vagueness of the term "higher power," the twelve steps are inherently biblical in their approach to life.

10. *Psychiatric-psychologic assessment and treatment capabilities.* While substance abuse is a disease process in its own right, it is well known that a wide variety of mental-illness conditions can coexist with substance abuse, often hidden under the more visible problem of the addiction to the drug. Recovering addicts who display erratic behaviors, psychosis, phobias, severe depression, impaired intellectual functioning, eating disorders, or anxiety states should be evaluated for the possibility of a coexisting psychiatric condition which may require treatment as well. A good treatment program can treat both an addiction problem and a psychiatric problem simultaneously if necessary.

11. *Insight-oriented therapy.* The disease of substance addiction has many facets. It is common for the recovering addict to need to address some very deep personality disorders in areas of self-esteem, personal identity, guilt, shame, inadequacy, and fear. These are issues that are not readily accessible in "task-oriented" therapy. The better programs will provide patients with access to trained counselors (and possibly process-oriented group therapy) in deep therapy on appropriate personality issues. This, of course, must not take the place of the primary emphasis of the program on addressing the addiction. But insight-oriented therapy can play an important complementary role.

12. *Provision for recreation, exercise, relaxation training and leisure activities.* The process of recovery for the addict will be greatly enhanced if adequate amount of time and assistance is provided for exercise and recreation. This will augment the rest of the treatment program. Many addicts have not been able to feel relaxed without a chemical in their system for years. The teaching of self-relaxation training exercises to patients by experienced staff members can give them a much-needed natural way to relax tired muscles and frazzled nerves without the use of any chemical substance.

13. *Vocational rehabilitation emphasis.* The better programs make a dedicated effort to assist their patients to reenter their chosen vocations as soon as possible. Whether

attending school, working nine to five, being a homemaker, or doing something else, the recovering addict needs to rebuild a productive self-esteem through personal accomplishments. The encouragement of active participation in church responsibilities and activities is also an essential component of this "vocational" emphasis. Whenever possible, it is helpful to enlist the support and participation of the patient's employer, teacher, or pastor in assisting the patient to stay active in the treatment disciplines (especially after discharge from an inpatient program).

14. *A strong commitment to aftercare.* Unfortunately, the tendency of recovering addicts is to relapse within a year of completing their treatment program unless a well-designed, intense, and accountable aftercare program is provided. A two-year aftercare plan with regular meetings is ideal for following up patients after the inpatient treatment program. (Outpatient treatment programs require at least as long a routine follow-up of recovery.) Since drug use affects every area of the patients' lives, good programs assist in reconstructing each area, including spiritual maturity, school, work, friendships, family relationships, and the use of leisure time.

15. *Commitment to the twelve-step process.* The oldest and most proven are the twelve steps of Alcoholics Anonymous. As we have noted, a number of Christians have difficulty with AA because of its vague reference to a "higher power." AA's steps are inherently biblical, and can still serve as the basis for guiding the recovering addict's treatment.

CONCLUSION

Is there any evidence to show the benefits of treatment? The least valuable testimony is that of the drug users themselves. However, behavior speaks loudly—louder than mere words.

General Motors found that at one plant absenteeism and payment of medical benefits due to alcoholism decreased at least 80 percent in a group of employees who underwent active treatment of their alcoholism. In another plant whose alcoholics did not receive treatment these same statistics more than doubled.[2]

Substance addiction is a disease that takes the very best of effort from those who treat it and a commitment to persevere from those receiving the treatment, if success is to be achieved. What is success in drug treatment? It is drug-free living, responsible living, and being happier drug-free than when addicted. There is no such thing as an addict who is beyond hope. Recovery is *always* possible, because what is impossible with man is possible with God.

CHAPTER TEN

WORKING WITH SUBSTANCE-ABUSE FAMILIES

COUNSELING AND PREVENTION

YOU MAY OR MAY NOT HAVE HAD EXPERIENCE in counseling the substance-abuse family. In this first section of this chapter, we will give an overview of general counseling principles and referral guidelines. We will then discuss codependency and spirituality. In the last section, we will discuss prevention principles which will be helpful to counselors in working with families in the congregation and/or community.

COUNSELING THE SUBSTANCE-ABUSE FAMILY

Chapter 6 discussed the effects of substance abuse on the family system. It is important that we keep this fact in mind—

we are counseling a family system even though the presenting client may be a lone individual. The level of intrapersonal pain of this family member has reached an intolerable level, causing him or her to reach out for help. And though at first you see only the client, you may be assured that the entire family is affected.

As a pastoral counselor it can be surprisingly easy to find oneself trapped in the "rescue" role when counseling the substance-abuse family. Out of a motivation of love, but without knowing the manipulative denial behaviors of these family systems, the inexperienced pastoral counselor is in a very vulnerable position clinically. One of the best preventative measures is to arm oneself with knowledge about the addiction process and codependency theory. Asking for help from other professionals in the substance-abuse therapy field is certainly no measure of failure! Instead, it is an opportunity to expand your clinical skills. Your effectiveness can do nothing but improve if you know what you are looking for.

A wise counselor also is aware of his or her limitations. *Know when to refer.* Be aware of the treatment facilities in your area. Make an appointment with the director of counseling there. Be aware of the self-help groups in your area, such as AA, Al-Anon, and others. Pastors might consider opening their church buildings as meeting places for family members affected by substance abuse. Recovery is a spiritual journey; what better place than the church as a location for this ministry?

CLINICAL INTERVENTIONS WITH MANIPULATIVE FAMILY SYSTEMS

In chapter 8 we discussed the cycle of codependency. Now we want to discuss some specific "games" that families and/or individuals may use to avoid dealing with therapy issues. We will also discuss how you as a counselor can assist the counselee in recognizing these games, and cancel or alter them for a healthier response.

"Gotcha"

"Gotcha" is a game in which the individual or the family as a system demonstrates behavior that might be threatening to the counselor. Such behavior may be a direct threat, but is more likely to be of a more subtle nature. It may include a questioning of your competence or motives, including sexual innuendoes, or simple comments about your own personal behavior.

The payoff of this game for the counselee is to temporarily feel superior to you, the counselor, by having successfully raised your anxiety level. But the long-term payoff is *guilt* from having done this. This feeds the guilt/punishment cycle as discussed in chapter 4, which of course feeds the addiction and codependency cycles.

The clinical intervention for this game is for you to take the focus off of yourself and remind them of why they came to you in the first place. Then explore with the clients their motivation for their statement, helping them understand the difference between their negative behavior and their personal worth as persons created by God. Assist the individual in the system to recognize and discriminate between appropriate and inappropriate guilt.

"Save Me—Save Me"

In this game the family system acts as if it is totally unable to function without complete, direct advice from the counselor. The statement heard most from these families is: "just tell me what to do" and the implication is "so that everything will be alright." The counselor who is inexperienced, wanting to help the family, may comply wholeheartedly and spell out in detail what the family "needs to do" to secure recovery. Of course, and often to the surprise of the counselor, the individual or family system has no intention of following through. The payoff of this game for the counselees is to reinforce the negative belief system: "See, we are no good. We couldn't even follow your good advice." This attitude and belief reinforces the addiction behavior pattern. Some of this may be beyond the conscious awareness of the counselee.

To intervene with this game, do not give very much direct advice. Explore options with the family, but allow them to make the choices. Be sure the members are aware of your support, but assist them in seeing with clarity that the responsibility for choice or change is with them, and begin or go on with your counseling.

"Punish Us, Please"

In this game the family responses can be really chaotic. They violate almost all of the contracts you have assisted in developing. They will not abide by the family conjoint "rules," such as no physical acting out during sessions. (This is not to be confused with a true loss-of-control situation.) It is almost as if the family has a prearranged negative script that is well practiced. It is as if they are asking for you to "kick them out" of therapy.

The payoff for the counselees of this game is to reinforce an unhealthy need to be punished, and to give credence to their false belief that they are unable to change. Intervention with such a family system can be attempted by exploring this payoff with them. Observe how the power of the family system is distributed during these sessions. The counselor must assume a very firm, but kind, position. Help them to set very concrete short-term goals and begin, or go on with counseling.

"One and Only"

This game can be very flattering to the counselor. The family takes a position that no one nor anything else on the face of the earth can help them as much as the counselor. These families refuse to attend any self-help groups, such as AA or Al-Anon. They may refuse to follow up on any referral to any other professional, clinic, or treatment facility. The payoff of this game for the counselee is the maintenance of the denial system. If the family is not exposed to confrontation or other professional change agents, they will not recognize a need to change their behavior. Also, the addicted family system may resist any type of group experience. This may be out of a fear of change or a sense of shame that they feel from society, which tells them (they think) drug abuse is a worse sin than any other.

The counselor's intervention for this family system is to reflect back to them that if they have so much confidence in you, surely they will follow through with your recommendations. Take them with you step by step through the above payoff. Be careful of the flattery, even if the family uses your ministerial position as the reason. If you are placed on a pedestal by the family you have but one direction to go from there—down. Contract with them for some small participation effort on their part and begin or go on with your counseling.

"Dr. Freud"

This game is well played by the professional person although it is not limited to the college-educated. The family system sounds, in session, like a university lecture in Psychology 101. By that we mean every verbalization is intellectualized. These families can repeat the concepts of addiction and codependency without error. However, nothing seems to be coming from "below the neck." It is very easy to believe that they are doing well in therapy, because they sound "so good." They tell you about emotions; they don't share with much affect what they are feeling. The payoff for them is to avoid looking at what hurts. How this plays into the addiction cycle is obvious. The unprocessed emotions that are allowed to build lead to a painful reality that is either drugged by continual substance abuse or used in the codependency cycle.

These families are very threatened by emotions of any variety. They have a difficult time even recognizing, much less processing, emotions. Gestalt or experiential therapy which reflects back the intellectualization with gradual progression toward expressing feelings that seem safe to the family, can be helpful. Sentence-completion questions may also be helpful.

Games can be used alone or in combination by both individuals and family systems. As a counselor, being aware of them and being able to assist your clients to healthier behaviors is both a challenging and rewarding experience.

Dr. Edward Kaufman, a professor of psychiatry and human behavior at the University of California, discussed the importance of working with the family systems in a recent article:

What has frequently been neglected is the importance of involving the three-generational family system, including children and the alcoholic's parents and in-laws, in order to change the family sufficiently to stop the alcoholic's drinking and hopefully restore family homeostasis.[1]

149

Even if it is not possible for you to achieve multigenerational participation, the concepts of family-system dynamics must be included in working with the family of the substance abuser. With this approach both the clinician and client will have a higher rate of success, and the family cycle of addiction can be broken.

It is indeed an exciting time to be involved in the treatment of substance abusers for we are in the "courtship" phase of the impending marriage of family-system theory and addictionology. As our research efforts increase and our knowledge base expands, perhaps the gifts and blessings of more complete recovery strategies will be ours for future generations.

CODEPENDENCY AND SPIRITUALITY

There is a very significant connection between codependency and spirituality. Timmen Cermak, M.D., in his book on codependency makes these observations concerning family-system dysfunction:

> For the purpose of clinical assessment of individual clients, codependency can best be seen as a disease entity. CD [chemical dependency] therapists speak of family members as being affected by codependence, or as being actively codependent. Such assessments imply that a consistent pattern of traits and behaviors is recognizable across individuals, and that these traits and behaviors can create significant dysfunction.[2]

The counseling field holds a variety of views on the exact definition and parameters of codependency. Whatever the final clinical definition evolves into, it is obvious that in such cases the family system is dysfunctional and certain observable patterns of behavior are seen (see chapter 8).

We suggest that codependency is any pathological bonding process that results in a learned behavior and belief system which contains oppressive rules with painful consequences. The spiritual life of codependent individuals is significantly affected. One example of concern here is the substance abuser. Any individual who bonds to a substance abuser may develop

150

codependency behaviors. This could include grandchildren, co-workers, or even members of the same church. All that is required is a significant bond.

We are learning that many individuals in the helping professions have codependency families of origin. It is assumed that such professionals often choose the "family hero" role and a service-oriented vocation due to unresolved issues of childhood.

Because the codependent system is a *dysfunctional* system, there are often family secrets, specific role assignments that are required to maintain the unhealthy family dynamics, and conditional love. Life becomes unpredictable and emotionally unsafe. (See chapter 6 for further discussion.)

The emotional hallmarks of this system are *shame* and *guilt*. Shame is about who you are (being). Guilt is about what you do or say (actions). Individuals coming from such systems carry these two burdens deeply within themselves. Shame and guilt keep people separated from the love of Christ and from others. Individuals are trapped in the codependency cycle. Codependent individuals see themselves as "bad" people. They are ill both emotionally and spiritually. Their emotional thought processes are impaired and they separate themselves from their own spiritual power and from the spiritual power available to them in Jesus Christ.

How does the codependent individual get well? As with the addict, healing is a life-long process. There are twelve-step programs available for codependents. Adequate, healing therapy for codependents includes:

1. confrontation of the impaired thinking,
2. therapeutic discharge of the repressed emotions in a safe environment,
3. processing the grief over lost relationships or a childhood,
4. finding and nurturing the inner child, and
5. accepting the grace of Jesus Christ, their Higher Power.

Only then can codependent individuals become who they were created to be. Individuals cannot go back and change their actions of the past, but they can change how they perceive the past. The repentance process provides the avenue of freeing one's self from the guilt of past actions. Paul spoke of the difference between "godly sorrow" and worldly sorrow (2 Cor. 7:9, 10). Godly sorrow leads to repentance and growth from one's errors. This is the appropriate guilt, as discussed in chapter 4. However, worldly sorrow is akin to the inappropriate guilt explained in that chapter. This inappropriate guilt leads to self-punishing behaviors which foster separation from others and God. This is the death so clearly stated in verse 10: "but worldly sorrow brings death." *Receiving and accepting the forgiveness of Christ which is so freely given allows an individual to begin again to trust self and others.*

For those who use the twelve-step method in their programs, step 2, 3, and 4 worksheets—the spiritual inventory and the character inventory—are presented below. These have been adapted from William Springborn's book *Foundations of Recovery.*[3] Catherine Samb, M.S., and Scott Washburn, Th.M., both substance-abuse counselors at Memorial Hospital in Garland, Texas, developed this adaptation.

Spiritual Inventory
Second- and Third-Step Worksheet

1. What is God like, according to your own understanding? Do you think of him as critical or nurturing; as judgmental or forgiving; as distant or close to you? What feelings do you have when you talk (pray) to him?
2. What are your responsibilities in working on your recovery? How does God play a role in your recovery? Make a list comparing your responsibilities and God's role in your recovery.
3. What does it mean to you "to trust" or "to turn over" something to God? How will you know by your behavior and feelings whether or not you are "turning over" your addiction to God?
4. What priority (or importance) do you give to God in your life? What areas of your life in addition to your addiction can you "turn over" to God?
5. What does the Serenity Prayer mean to you? How does it fit into your recovery?

Character Inventory
Fourth-Step Worksheet

1. List any resentments which you still have.
2. List any character defects which apply to you. Define each of them in your own words (keep it simple) and briefly describe specific examples of each from your own experience. Discuss how you plan to change each of them a day at a time.
3. Look at your resentments together with your character defects. Discuss how you see that your character defects may have played a part in harboring your resentments. Discuss how you see that your addiction along with your character defects interfered with healthy relationships. Are your resentments justified or unjustified (examine each one)?
4. List any character assets (positive character traits) which apply to you. Define each of them in your own words (keep it simple) and list examples of each from your own experience.

PREVENTION STRATEGIES

It would be wonderful if we had a vaccine that would drug-proof our families. But that is unrealistic. It would be nice if "just say no" strategies were learned and used by all adolescents, and if all adults were abstinent or temperate drinkers. But once again, the world is not like that.

He is running a little late, but then Forest Searls Tennant, M.D., one of medicine's leading experts in the fight against drug abuse, is never early. . . . This day, dressed in one of his many varieties of a gray suit with striped tie, he arrives at his storefront office in West Covina, Calif., wearing a perplexed look:

"They've sent me an 18-year-old boy hooked on coke (cocaine)," he explains. "The parents are pleading with me to get the kid clean, and do you know what the kid says his major motivation is? His parents have had to promise to buy him a new $60,000 sports car to persuade him to make the effort. Brother! This is the drug problem in a

COUNSELING FOR SUBSTANCE ABUSE AND ADDICTION

nutshell. People don't know how to handle leisure time, how to handle boredom. People have forgotten how to entertain themselves, how to talk to each other. What's left are drugs."[4]

The problem of drug abuse and the solutions to it are much more complex. "At no time in world history has drug addiction been greater. Or growing faster. At no time in world history have traffickers been so rich. Or getting richer."[5]

The family still offers the best antidote to the problem of drug addiction. Even in urban ghetto areas, a strong family has been found to be a deterrent to drug use. Dr. Tennant further said:

I spent about a half-million of the public's tax dollars to learn what common sense could have told me. The people who get addicted to hard drugs share three childhood characteristics—they started smoking before they were 15; they were never taken to church; and they were seldom spanked. Today, I tell the parents' groups I address to do three things: "Tell your kids not to smoke, take them to church, and teach them discipline."[6]

As a counselor or pastor you may be called upon to present prevention strategies in your congregation or community. We hope this section of the book will give you some ideas and guidelines in working with families and discussing family-living concepts of drug prevention.

In order to resist this ever-increasing menace, the family needs to develop certain foundations or "pillars" that build family strength. This foundation allows the family members to survive the stresses and problems that we all encounter. The total absence of stress, or its opposite—the unremitting presence of stress—leads to problems. We need to have some degree of stress and some problems in order to grow. The following are pillars that are important in building a strong and healthy family.

Character foundations
Healthy peer associations
Spiritual depth
Family bonds
Personal achievement
Information and awareness

CHARACTER FOUNDATIONS

A child needs to develop in seven major areas in order to build a solid character foundation.

Self-Esteem

A child must develop a healthy self-concept or self-esteem. The beginnings of self-esteem are laid down in earliest childhood. Its development depends upon the relationship between parent and child. Though the following may seem elementary, they are crucial to developing this healthy relationship.

- Parents must take the time to talk *with* the children. If the children feel that what they have to say is important, then they will feel that they are significant and worthwhile.
- A parent (or parents) should provide encouragement and enthusiasm for the interests and accomplishments of the children. They will not put them down or belittle them because their plans and ideas aren't the same as theirs.
- A parent (or parents) provides children with opportunities to explore, to be curious, and to be creative. But the parents must be prepared for and be willing to allow a certain amount of messiness.
- A parent (or parents) allows children to be emotionally spontaneous, not denying the normal feelings they have. They will help them to maintain a balance between self-control and self-expression.
- A parent (or parents) encourages children in their games of pretend or fantasy, allowing them to stay busy and be creative—an important cure for boredom. Boredom is a major factor in why kids try drugs.

- A parent (or parents) allows children to assume a share of the decision-making in the home, letting them have input in choosing what will be done during family activities.
- A parent (or parents) understands how to set limits and utilize discipline as necessary. Children derive a great sense of security from knowing that the parents are in charge. Being able to say no and "blame" it on the parents makes it easier for children to resist peer pressure.

Responsibility

This was easier to develop in our children when the cows had to be milked and the garden had to be tended so that everyone could eat. Today, our modern conveniences have eliminated many of our daily tasks. It is now much harder to teach personal responsibility. By giving children assigned tasks and holding them accountable for their completion, parents can still teach them personal responsibility. A parent should let the children know that they appreciate their kids' efforts. Also, keeping them busy will give them less time to waste and make them less likely to experiment with drugs.

Respect for Others

In the past, children would not even consider talking back to a teacher or an adult. Times have changed. This is now the norm! Remind parents to teach their children to respect other people, to listen to them, to acknowledge that they are worthwhile, and that they can indeed learn from them.

Decision Making

If a parent provides all of the answers and solutions for the children, they will never be able to make decisions for themselves. Encourage parents not to try to shield the children from the consequences of their bad decisions—this is how they will learn to make better decisions. An individual who feels comfortable and confident in his or her ability to make decisions will be better equipped to handle the stresses and problems of life (including the temptation to use drugs).

Acceptance and Expression of Feelings

We have said that drug abuse is a "disease of the feelings." Whether we feel good or bad, our feelings are real and need to be expressed and acknowledged. A parent needs to listen to the children and allow them to express their feelings. This is very important. However, there are both healthy and unhealthy ways to express feelings. By accepting the children's feelings and teaching them how to deal with those feelings, a parent can train them so they will be less likely to express their feelings through unhealthy behavior, such as using drugs.

Learning Healthy Problem Solving

Life is full of problems. But the parent knows that it is how the children handle them that makes the difference between happiness and despair, success and failure. If they don't teach their children how to handle them, the youngsters will develop some unhealthy and self-destructive behaviors. Parents may need reminding to be realistic with the children—some days will be better than others, and some problems will not have easy solutions.

The Ability to Say No

The children need the ability to maintain convictions and deal with difficult situations that threaten their value system or integrity. Parents can prepare children to resist the pressures that our culture places upon them, knowing that an individual who has learned how to deal with difficult situations will be far less likely to use drugs as a way of coping.

HEALTHY PEER ASSOCIATIONS

Why is peer acceptance so important and why is peer pressure so hard to resist? The answer is because many families have allowed peer relationships to become stronger and more important than parent-child relationships.

This begins during the kindergarten years, when children become involved in activities outside the home. Some children are never home; they are always at music lessons, sports activities, scouting, social functions, or at friends' homes. In time, their peers become the dominant persons in their lives and the parents become just the means to provide these activities. When the normal period of teenage rebellion hits, the parents are viewed as hostile strangers who have no right to tell the child what to do.

We suggest the following as antidotes for peer pressure and as guides to help the children form healthy peer relationships. Parents should:

- limit outside activities.
- make the home a place where the kids enjoy spending time, a place where they want to bring their friends.
- spend the time that is needed to make their relationship with the children the most meaningful and most important to them.
- know their child's friends by name and talk with them whenever they visit. They should view them as a valuable asset to their children.
- know about the character of their child's friends, and not be afraid to ask other parents.
- practice what they preach. Parents will not want to have close friends whom they wouldn't bring home to meet the children.

SPIRITUAL DEPTH

The conduct of a parent's spiritual life has the most important influence on the child's developing personal relationship with God. As Thoreau said, "What you are speaks so loudly, I can't hear a word that you are saying." In counseling, we should frankly ask parents: "Is your relationship with God the foundation upon which you are building your life?" "Do you spend time every day in prayer and Bible study?" "Are you depending upon God to meet your needs?" "Are you trusting in him to lead you through the difficulties encountered in daily living?" "Are you spending time teaching your child about God by reading the Bible with him or her?" If parents can say yes to these questions, they are giving their children the best environment in which to grow spiritually.

What role does the church play in this process? The church

needs to support the parents in their efforts. It needs to provide an atmosphere that encourages spiritual growth in the entire family. It needs to model biblical living. And it should be a place of activities offering healthy alternatives to that of drugs and our hedonistic culture.

FAMILY BONDS

Families which have strong interpersonal ties and experience a deep sense of "bondedness" are a formidable source of strength for the young person who is seeking to resist the pressures of the peer culture. Everyone wants to have a healthy and strong family, but what are the attributes of such a family?

Author and nationally recognized columnist Dolores Curran, in preparing the research for her book, *Traits of a Healthy Family,* gathered information from hundreds of families and was able to isolate fifteen characteristics which repeatedly surfaced in the healthy families. These fifteen traits are a portrait of the healthy family.

1. *Communicates and listens.* Strong families recognize nonverbal messages, encourage individual feelings and independent thinking, and discourage turn-off words and put-down phrases.

2. *Affirms and supports one another.* These families practice the art of praising one another and helping one another without being asked, and of being able to share credit with one another for accomplishments. Such families place a premium on being able to work together as a team.

3. *Teaches respect for others.* These families teach respect for all humans regardless of background, race, or religious preference. They respect one another as God's creations and see abuse of the person or misuse of someone's property as alien to the basic value system of the family.

4. *Develops a sense of trust.* Healthy families demonstrate trust, especially between husband and wife; infidelity between marital partners just doesn't exist in generally healthy families. The family regularly demonstrates that family members are to be believed and accepted at face value. Deceit is seen as a serious violation of the family code.

5. *Has a sense of play and humor.* Healthy families work at creating activities that are enjoyable, and also derive plenty of enjoyment just by relaxing and being around one another. The children develop at any early age a sense of permission and acceptance concerning playfulness and spontaneous enjoyment of life. Parents who are too serious and distracted by the cares of this world drain the family dry of its natural spontaneity.

6. *Exhibits a sense of shared responsibility.* Responsibility involves not only taking care of assigned tasks and meeting explicit family demands. It also entails responding to the moods of others and doing the extra little things, often with no recognition, which make the home happier.

7. *Teaches a sense of right and wrong.* Healthy families communicate a solid and dependable value system to their children. Such values are 10 percent "taught" (by instructions from the parents) and 90 percent "caught" (by observing what values the parents actually live by).

8. *Has a strong sense of family in which rituals and traditions abound.* Healthy families have many family traditions which revolve around special dates, remembered events, and meaningful times which the family has shared together. Shirley Dobson and Gloria Gaither, in their excellent book *Let's Make a Memory*, show how to develop memories that will help knit the family together emotionally and serve as a bonding point through the years.[7]

9. *Has a balance of interaction among members.* In healthy families, no one person "hogs" all the attention or dominates the home. Members are allowed to share opinions and are afforded the inherent worth of recognition and appreciation.

10. *Has a shared religious core.* Strong families have a shared faith and participate regularly in church activities. Their relationship to God, however, goes deeper than just going to church and is the basis for their strength as a family.

11. *Respects the privacy of one another.* Members of healthy families don't take one another for granted. A sense of personal respect for one another's property, feelings, and preferences exists in the family.

12. *Values service to others.* Healthy families appreciate the value of other people and are willing to serve others. They

are community-minded and respond to the pain and need of other families whenever able.

13. *Fosters family mealtime and* Curran states the "families who do a good job of communicating make the dinner meal an important part of the day." When a family sits together for meals it is more than simply a time of eating together; rather, it is a time for sharing of ideas and feelings and important events of the day.

14. *Shares leisure time.* We have all heard the phrase, "the family that prays together, stays together," but it may be just as well said that "the family that *plays* together, stays together." The family that can't enjoy playing together during the good times will have a hard time communicating with one another during the times of stress.

15. *Admits to and seeks help with problems.* In healthy families, members are not defensive or turned off by honest feedback and suggestions. They can discuss problems openly. They expect problems as a normal part of family life and develop ways to deal with them.

PERSONAL ACHIEVEMENT

It has been said that drugs fill a vacuum in a young person's life. If drug use is to be prevented, then this vacuum must be filled with healthy activities. If a person has no sense of purpose, the vacuum will again reemerge when a person becomes drug-free. Thus finding something to live for is essential to a person's recovery from addiction.

Through worthwhile achievements adolescents learn many of the skills that they will need in adult life. They learn how to solve problems, how to make and to use money, how to work with and get along with others, and how to stick with a task even though it is difficult. In the process, self-esteem and the right kind of self-confidence develop. The converse is true—drug use severely retards and damages growth in this area. Parents can encourage their children toward personal achievement in several ways. You as a counselor can advise them:

- Help your child become involved in worthwhile projects and activities, but limit those to the things that will help develop character.

- Praise your child for his or her participation in the activity, not simply for achieving success.
- Make your home a place where your children have as much fun with the family (and with friends) as they can with outside activities.
- Plan projects and activities in which parent and child work together. This helps develop perseverance, commitment, and a sense of accomplishment.
- Don't over-indulge your child in an attempt to either compensate for your shortcomings as a parent or to make up for the deprivations of your childhood.

INFORMATION AND AWARENESS

"I wish that I had heard this when I was a kid," was the comment of a former drug user when asked what would be a good way to educate the kids of today about drugs. He lamented the fact that in the late 1960s (when he started using pot) no public information was available about the dangers of drugs.

Much good information is now in circulation about the use and abuse of drugs; parents and their children need to be informed. Appendix 3 lists books and organizations that the authors recommend.

Education about drugs needs to be factual and believable. Scare tactics do not work—in fact they may increase the natural curiosity of a teen or a child about drugs. One way to educate children about drug abuse is for the parents to read and discuss news articles about drug abuse with their children. Stories are in newspapers and magazines, and on TV news almost daily. The news media have done an excellent job of late in presenting both the dangers and the scope of the drug-abuse epidemic engulfing Western society.

Another good way for parents to increase their children's awareness is for them to obtain literature (written for the young person) from local drug education organizations. This literature should educate young people concerning the why of drugs, their dangers, and how to resist drugs.

Parents can also find out what resources are available and get qualified speakers to come to the school and church.

Finally, the best education is that of the parents' example.

Adults who care about their children don't take drugs themselves, except as prescribed by a physician for illness. If they are always taking pills, their children get the message: Drug use is the norm. Many parents of teens have discovered that their voluntary abstinence from alcohol does far more than any lecture about the dangers of alcohol.

Parents should discuss with their children, in advance, situations in which drug use will arise. The children *will* be offered drugs, and planning ahead will make it easier for them to say no. According to Mary Doyen of the Colorado Health Department, children need to be taught refusal skills if they are to be able to say no to drugs. Some school districts in Colorado are teaching these skills beginning in kindergarten.[8]

Despite their typical resistance to parental authority, teens both want and need for the parent to be firm on this issue. This makes them feel secure in the parent's love and allows them to say no to their peers without losing face.

Here are some questions parents can discuss with their children:

Which of your friends will offer you drugs?

When will the offer likely be made?

Why are they using drugs in the first place?

How has drug use harmed them?

Why do they want you to use drugs with them?

What will they say to you in order to get you to give in?

What should you do when this happens?

The final aspect of awareness is: What is going on in our neighborhood, our schools and our community? Drug abuse will be battled most successfully at the community level, and, more specifically, family by family. The key to winning this battle is to reduce the demand for drugs, and this means changes in attitudes and values. As Christians, the "salt of the earth" and "light of the world," we have an active part to play.

Many communities have made great strides in reducing drug use. But this has only come after much hard work by law enforcement agencies, local government, community agencies, conscientious employers, concerned school officials, and—last but not least—parents. Most importantly, the parents were willing to "network" together and establish an environment in which drug-free was the norm, rather than the exception. Many excellent guides to this process are listed in Appendix 3.

Finally, we present a satiric but useful list of all-too-frequent parental attitudes and behaviors which can lead children in the path of drug abuse. As the counselor, you may often refer parents to this list. You may want to have it available as a printed handout for parents whom you counsel. Most of us see ourselves in at least one of them. This list, which is adapted and has been used in the TOUCH program several years, is not intended to make people feel guilty, but rather to serve as a friendly reminder to those going through the trials of parenting. As they get caught up in the details of life, they sometimes don't notice harmful attitudes and habits that have crept in.

16 WAYS TO ENCOURAGE YOUR CHILD TO USE DRUGS

1. Never eat together as a family.
2. Never have family traditions which occur weekly, monthly, or annually that children can look forward to.
3. Never listen to your children; talk at them, but not with them.
4. Never let your children experience cold, fatigue, adventure, injury, risk, challenge, experimentation, failure, frustration, discouragement, etc.
5. Teach them to "do as I say, not as I do."
6. Leave the responsibility of spiritual training and development to the schools and the church, but don't teach them at home.
7. When confronted with the choice of whether spending time and money on a material pursuit or on a family activity, always choose the material.
8. Expect your children to achieve, to win, but don't teach them the principles of life, of living. Let them learn them on their own.
9. Take a "pick-me-up pill" in the morning, followed by a "relaxant" at night.

10. Never correct your children appropriately, but uphold them before the law, school, church, and friends as "not *my* child."
11. Undermine the role of the father in the home—never allow the father's influence in the home. Stay together for the sake of the children—or better yet, get a divorce.
12. Always pick up after the child; never let the child take any responsibility.
13. Keep your home atmosphere in a state of chaos.
14. Always solve their problems and make their decisions for them.
15. Be too busy with business, civic, church, or social life to spend time with your children. Or when you do have the time, spend it together, watching television.
16. Don't teach them while they are young. Wait until they are old enough to learn so they can decide right and wrong for themselves.

CHAPTER ELEVEN

QUESTIONS AND ANSWERS ABOUT DRUG ABUSE

THE PROBLEM OF SUBSTANCE ABUSE is complex and difficult. We have tried to provide a framework for understanding the abuser and his or her world. On the following pages is a sampling of the most common questions about substance abuse.

Why do children from Christian families get into drugs?
Being raised in a Christian home is no guarantee that a person will not try drugs. This may be due to curiosity, peer pressure, a desire to escape, rebellion, or some other reason. Unfortunately, once a person tries drugs the desire to continue may be irresistible. Parents must remember that the drug-using adolescent has made the choice to try drugs and then to

continue using them. They should not feel guilty or blame themselves.

What does the Bible say about drug abuse?

Beginning with the book of Genesis, the Bible shows how alcohol caused problems in the lives of both Noah and Jacob. The problems related to drunkenness are well detailed in the book of Proverbs. In the New Testament, Paul condemns the drunkenness that was common in his time (as in ours) because of the problems that it caused believers.

Other drugs, such as marijuana, cocaine, or hallucinogens, are not specifically mentioned. However, sorcery, which was very common in Bible times, is condemned, and sorcerers frequently used drugs to intoxicate and then control individuals. The word for sorcery comes from the Greek word *pharmakia*, which is the root of our English word *pharmacy*.

I've been using pot on and off for years and it is not a problem for me. If alcohol is okay in the Bible, why is it wrong to use pot or other drugs?

In Ephesians 5:18, we are told, "Do not get drunk on wine, which leads to debauchery. Instead, be filled with the Spirit." This is really a problem of control—is one controlled by wine or by God's Holy Spirit? It is possible to use alcohol and not be controlled by it. However, in order to get high from all other drugs of abuse, you must become intoxicated, which means being under the drug's control.

My father is an alcoholic. Will I become one?

We know that children of alcoholics can inherit a genetic tendency to also become alcoholics. That means that if they start to use alcohol they may have a compulsion (caused by their brain chemistry) to continue and to increase the amount that they drink. If you grow up with an alcoholic parent (or parents), you will be affected by the abnormal behavior. This could cause you to follow in your parent's footsteps, even though you dislike what your parent did. If you have an alcoholic parent, the best advice is *don't start drinking* yourself!

Can you explain what a heavy drinker is?

A heavy drinker is someone who drinks regularly and who drinks until he or she becomes intoxicated. Just a six-pack of beer will cause many people to become intoxicated, even though they may appear to act fairly normal.

What are the warning signs of drug abuse?

These are covered in Appendix 4.

What about steroids?

Steroids are not mood-altering or addictive drugs. However, they are being used increasingly by young athletes to improve their performance and amount of muscle tissue. Chronic use of steroids has led to dangerous effects—harmful mood swings, poor wound healing, increased risk of bone or joint injury due to excessive muscle tissue, decreased sex drive, and urinary tract difficulties. They are not harmless!

Is caffeine (and caffeine pills) addictive?

Caffeine is a mild stimulant and is the most widely used drug in the world. It is found in coffee, most cola beverages, chocolate, cocoa, tea, caffeine pills, and in many over-the-counter pain medications. It is also addictive, just like any other mood-altering drug. Additionally, excessive use is now linked to heart disease in men and fibrocystic breast disease in women.[1]

How much is safe? Two cups of coffee (300 mg.) per day, or the equivalent, is felt to be safe. From two to five cups per day is in the gray zone. Over five cups a day is both addictive and associated with a doubling of the risk of death from heart attack. Caffeine withdrawal symptoms include: sleepiness, fatigue, irritability, and a craving for coffee (or other source of caffeine).

Is it wrong for Christians to drink alcoholic beverages?

The Bible condemns drunkenness, but not using alcohol itself, despite the claims of some Christians. However, you are no doubt well aware of the risks and problems associated with alcohol. You need to help individuals make their decision based upon their family history of alcohol problems, what they use alcohol for, and what effect that use of alcohol might have upon others. We now know that children who grow up in homes which are very rigid and where alcohol use is condemned (we are not talking about simple abstinence) are more likely to have problems with it or other addictions as adults than those in less rigid homes.

My dad drinks beer every day, but I've never seen him drunk. Is he an alcoholic?

An alcoholic is one who has to drink out of a compulsive desire or craving and cannot stop drinking voluntarily. Such a person will drink despite adverse consequences to his or her health, family, or financial situation brought on by the drinking.

Why can't people just stop drugs on their own? I think that they should be able to use their will power.

Once people are addicted, their brain chemistry is altered and they have an intense craving for the drug, despite their will power. If they are detoxified from a given drug, this craving will usually go away. However, once drug users are clean, they may well have a psychological craving that can be triggered by many cues (i.e., seeing someone light a "joint" or drink a beer). This is where prayer power and a good aftercare program are essential.

Are people who use drugs demon possessed?

Demon possession does not cause drug abuse. The effects of drug addiction are bad enough by themselves. Many times we would rather blame outside forces than take responsibility for our behavior or that of our loved ones. The authors have not seen documented demon possession and drug abuse. However, some of our patients have related their involvement with either Satan worship or witchcraft due to association with drug-using peers.

Are urine tests for drug use reliable?

Urine drug testing is a very reliable and accurate way to detect drug use—if it is done by competent people using the best equipment. At this time there is no standardization of test methods and no regulation or certification of drug-testing labs, as is required for other labs. Thus, questions are raised about the reliability of these tests.

The most common error in these labs is the *false-negative*, that is, a test that is really positive, but is reported as negative. A good lab will do a second test on any urine found to be positive for drugs before it reports a positive result. If a urine test is to be reliable, the specimen must be collected under observation. Otherwise, there is a likelihood of getting a fake specimen.

How can you help someone who doesn't want to be helped?

You can't. A person who is addicted has to want help before treatment can succeed. However, if a person can be committed for treatment (by intervention, see chapter 6), the person may well change his or her mind after becoming drug-free. Remember, though you may feel that the individual is beyond help, never quit praying for that person.

I have a friend who is using drugs. What can I do to help him?

Don't do anything that will enable him to continue to use drugs. Don't loan him money, don't bail him out of jail, don't let him tell you all his woes (this helps him to believe the lies that he is concocting). This sounds harsh, but you cannot show normal compassion to the drug user—he or she will only take advantage of it. You also must lovingly, but firmly, confront the person with the fact of his or her addiction and need for treatment.

Why should I help the drug user? After all, he brought it on himself.

We are all sinners and should not condemn others just because their sins are different than ours. In Galatians 6:1, 2 we are told "Brothers, if someone is caught in a sin, you who are spiritual should restore him gently. But watch yourself, or you also may be tempted. Carry each other's burdens, and in this way you will fulfill the law of Christ."

What happens to the baby when a pregnant woman takes drugs?

All of the drugs of abuse including alcohol will adversely affect the baby. The heroin addict's baby will be addicted and will have to be treated for withdrawal. Cocaine babies are high-strung and irritable for about six months after birth, and need extra nurturing. Babies of alcoholic mothers may have Fetal Alcohol Syndrome which includes retardation, irritability, and delayed mental and physical development. Women who are heavy smokers may have babies with lower birth weight and slower development.[2]

Can a person get AIDS from using drugs?

Yes. It can be transmitted by contaminated needles and syringes. You can also get it by sexual contact with an AIDS carrier. A fact that is often overlooked is that many people who are using drugs are involved with either prostitution or multiple sex partners. Drug use may also lower one's resistance to infections, including AIDS.

My husband will not give up alcohol, despite my pleading. Should I divorce him?

You and your family will be harmed emotionally if you stay in the present situation. You may have to separate from him for your own well-being and that of your children. This may help him decide to get treatment. Divorce should only be considered if all other efforts have failed, and after sound biblical counsel from a responsible Christian(s).

My father is an alcoholic and beats my mother and us children. Despite this, my mother won't leave him. Why?

Unfortunately, many women who are married to alcoholics have an unconscious need for punishment and can't leave their abusive husbands. Frequently, they grew up with an alcoholic father. Others may just feel trapped and are paralyzed into inaction. If you are being physically or sexually abused, get help now. If you know of child abuse, report it to your local child welfare authorities.

Once you become an addict, are you always an addict, even if you no longer use drugs?

Yes. You will run the risk of relapse if you take drugs or alcohol *even once.* That is why one must stay away from drugs and drug-using friends. If you have learned how to live and enjoy life without drugs and have a vital relationship with God, you have all the right ingredients for staying clean.

My best friend's parents let him (an adolescent) drink wine on special occasions. Will he become an alcoholic?

Many families do this. In some families in which moderate alcohol use is practiced, there may be less likelihood of the children becoming alcoholics. However, in many families that condone the teens' use of alcohol, this probably encourages them to drink more. The best advice from drug-abuse treatment experts is that teens should not be allowed to drink.

Why are people now saying that pot is harmful?

In the past, marijuana was not as potent as that now available. Additionally, research has helped us understand the dangers of pot. It contributes to chronic brain impairment, increased respiratory infections, decreased motor skills, amotivational syndrome, and addiction. Experience has shown that pot is not a safe drug at all. One never knows what any drug will do to his or her body.

What if I use pot or cocaine just for fun. Will I get hooked?

Many people believe that it is safe to use drugs from time to time ("recreational use"), and that they won't get hooked. The problem is that everyone who becomes addicted began as an occasional user. There is no way to predict who will progress from occasional use to addiction. Why take the chance?

Why do some people seem to be able to use drugs and not get addicted?

Some people do use drugs on a sporadic basis and don't seem to get hooked. They are the so-called "social users." Since these people don't seek treatment very often, we do not know what makes them different from the addict. We do know that many of them will go on to full-blown addiction. It is just a matter of time.

What happens when a person relapses? Is it hopeless?

If persons relapse they will quickly become physically addicted again. The sooner they quit the drug and seek treatment the fewer problems they will have. Many alcoholics and drug users will have temporary relapses, but will stay clean most of the time. It is not hopeless.

Why does it seem that drug abuse is getting worse?

The percentage of people using drugs has declined from a peak in 1979–80. However, the use of cocaine has dramatically risen since then. The media have been much more thorough in reporting drug abuse in the past two years. According to a report in *The New York Times* in late 1986, there is much more public awareness now of the hazards of drug abuse.

Are pep pills (amphetamines) dangerous?

Amphetamines work just like cocaine and are just as addicting. They do not have the stigma of cocaine because they are legal drugs (though usually illegally manufactured). Many people fall into abuse of these drugs because they take them to help weight loss and find that they like them. This also applies to over-the-counter diet pills which work similarly to amphetamines.

Will my child suffer permanent damage from taking drugs?

Your child may. It depends upon which drugs were used, at what age the drug use started, how often they were used, and what complications resulted (infection from contaminated needles, brain damage from overdose, etc.). Common problems include: thinking and motor impairment from pot; nasal damage from snorting cocaine; paranoid thinking from amphetamines, cocaine, and PCP; liver damage from alcohol; accidental injuries and unplanned pregnancy while under the influence of any drug.

How do you know if you are addicted to a drug?

If you can't do without it. If one finds that using the drug is causing him or her problems of any kind—i.e., at work, at home, at school, with a spouse or one's children, with money, or with the law. See the self-tests, Appendix 5 and Appendix 6.

What are designer drugs?

These are drugs that are derivatives of known or existing drugs. They are synthetic (not derived from natural substances, as are cocaine, alcohol, heroin, marijuana, and some of the hallucinogens) and are usually manufactured in clandestine laboratories. They tend to be extremely potent and dangerous. For example, a derivative of the narcotic fentanyl, 3—methyl fentanyl—is two thousand times more potent than morphine!

Does cigarette smoking really lead to use of other drugs?

Most people who become addicted to other drugs of abuse (remember, the nicotine in cigarettes is an addicting drug) have smoked cigarettes before they used any other drug. This does not mean that cigarette smoking will lead to use of other drugs, but it does mean "watch out." Many experts consider nicotine a "gateway" drug (see below).

If people use pot will they go on to use other drugs?

Most people who are addicted to other drugs (besides pot) started with pot. This does not mean that pot use causes one to use other drugs, but as Dr. Robert DuPont (former head of National Institute on Drug Abuse) has pointed out, smoking pot is a "gateway" to the use of other drugs.[3]

Does saying no to drugs really work?

Yes, if children are taught how to say no to their peers. This must begin early in life at the grade-school level. A strong parent-child relationship and support is essential. For more details see chapter 10.

Am I to blame if my kids use drugs?

Unfortunately, many children whose parents did their best have gotten into drugs. Parents should not blame themselves, as this makes it easier for the drug user to deny responsibility for his or her addiction. Drug addiction begins with the decision to try drugs for the first time.

I've found some strange devices in my child's room. How do I know if they are drug paraphernalia?

Contact your local drug awareness/education organization for help. If they can't help you, call the National Federation of Parents for Drug-Free Youth (NFP) at 1–800–554–KIDS.

My brother says that he "needs" drugs to feel normal. Is this true?

Most people addicted to drugs feel bad because of the effects of the drugs themselves, and not because they have an underlying psychiatric disorder. From 20 to 40 percent of substance abusers do have serious emotional problems and they may use drugs to make themselves feel better. However, self-medication is never a good idea; they really need appropriate treatment.

Can drug abuse cause depression or other emotional problems?

Very much so. Many substance abusers are very depressed when they enter treatment. The majority begin to feel much better once they have begun to detoxify from the drug. However, they may experience intermittent periods of depression after they have become clean. This is probably a side-effect of their previous drug use.

Do drug users need any antidepressants or tranquilizers?

These may be needed during the hospital stay or during detoxification. Some drug users may need antidepressant therapy after they are released from the hospital (antidepressants are not addicting). However, recovering drug users should not be given either tranquilizers or sleeping pills, because both tranquilizers and sleeping pills can be very addicting. Unfortunately, many recovered drug addicts have become addicted to these drugs because they were given to aid sleep and remove anxiety. A much better approach would be Bible study, prayer, meditation and counseling.

How does drug abuse affect sexuality?

It is commonly thought that both marijuana and cocaine are aphrodisiacs. However, this probably is due more to psychological expectations of the drug than actual drug effect. It is also well known that alcohol reduces inhibitions, including those relating to sex. While it does have this effect, alcohol also has the effect of impairing performance, especially with chronic use.

Ultimately, when one is drug-addicted, his or her major interest is in using the drug; frequently, the person may lose all interest in sex. When one becomes drug free, the sex drive will usually return to normal, but this may require months to years.

Why does our family doctor not think that my mother is an alcoholic? He won't help the family get her into treatment.

Unfortunately, most physicians do not receive any training in the diagnosis and treatment of substance abuse. Thus, they are ill-prepared to help their patients who are addicted. Most of us (including doctors) will deny the presence of addiction in friends or family and will usually find other reasons to explain away the problem rather than face up to it.

Are over-the-counter medications addicting?

Yes, they can be. The most commonly abused over-the-counter medication is diet pills. Taken in hopes of suppressing appetite and, therefore, losing weight, they contain a drug (phenylpropanolamine) that is similar to amphetamine, and which acts as a stimulant. Also seen is addiction to the alcohol in many medications, such as cough syrups or sleep aids.

APPENDIX 1

GLOSSARY OF TERMS

ABSTINENCE. Living without the use of mind-altering drugs.

ADDICTION. See dependence.

ADDICTIVE. Any psychoactive chemical that can cause compulsive use in the people taking it.

AFTERCARE. The continued recovery process, after discharge from an inpatient treatment program, for the alcoholic or drug user and family. Aftercare may include self-help groups, growth groups, individual counseling, or psychotherapy.

AFTERCARE GROUP. A group of recovering substance abusers that is led by a trained professional staff and/or volunteer to support the recovery process.

ALCOHOLICS ANONYMOUS (AA). Founded in 1935 by and for alcoholics, AA is the prototype (and largest) of the self-help groups. The twelve steps to recovery constitute the core of the AA program. Members of AA maintain sobriety by attending meetings, by following the spiritual path suggested in the twelve steps, and by sharing their experience with other alcoholics who are still suffering. It is estimated that more than 1.5 million alcoholics maintain their sobriety in more than thirty thousand groups nationwide in the U.S. AA is active around the world and has several affiliated groups.

   Al-Anon. A self-help organization for codependent relatives of alcoholics, usually the spouse or parents.

   Al-Ateen. Designed for the teenage children of alcoholics. Alcoholic teenagers go directly into AA.

Adult Children of Alcoholics (ACOA). A self-help program aiding adults with problems resulting from having alcoholic parents. Not for the treatment of alcoholism.

Cocaine Anonymous (CA). A new organization for cocaine abusers founded in 1983, based on the principles of AA.

Gamblers Anonymous (GA). Based on AA principles and designed for compulsive gamblers.

Narcotics Anonymous (NA). Similar to AA, but designed for narcotic drug abusers.

Nar-Anon. For the codependents of those with narcotic drug addiction.

ALCOHOLISM. The compulsive and continued use of alcohol in the face of adverse consequences: medical, legal, and financial problems; difficulty at school and/or work, and in interpersonal relationships.

AMOTIVATIONAL SYNDROME. A state of passive withdrawal from usual work, school, and recreational activities, usually accompanied by failure in school, at work, and at home, due to chronic, heavy marijuana use.

BIG BOOK. The guidebook written by active members of Alcoholics Anonymous describing the behavior and characteristics of alcoholics.

BLACKOUT. A temporary dulling of vision, or loss of consciousness and/or memory caused by drug or alcohol intoxication.

BOTTOMING-OUT. When one has reached a level of emotional, spiritual, and physical harm, due to drug abuse, which he or she can no longer tolerate.

CHRONIC. A persistent disease or dysfunction which is incurable. In alcoholism or other drug addiction, total abstinence will lead to recovery, but the disease persists. [One is still susceptible to addiction if drug use starts again.]

CODEPENDENT (E.G., COALCOHOLIC). An important individual in the life of a drug-dependent person whose behavior helps support or maintain the addiction.

CONCERNED/SIGNIFICANT OTHERS. Those individuals who have important, meaningful, or influential relationships with the alcoholic or other drug-dependent person (not necessarily related).

CONFRONTING. A technique of challenging another person's behavior and perception of reality.

CONNING. To lie, persuade, or cajole for the purpose of manipulation or deception.

CONTRACTING. An agreement between either a drug treatment program or counselor and the individual seeking help. *Treatment Contract:* an agreement between the drug-dependent person and a treatment program which specifies the behaviors, services, and payments which each will provide. *Contingency Contract:* an agreement between the drug-dependent person and a treatment program which specifies what will happen if a relapse or "slip" occurs. The intention is to discourage relapse through the anticipation of negative consequences.

CONTROLLING. Answering, explaining, interpreting, or otherwise making decisions for others that they should make for themselves.

CRISIS. Crucial point or event in the course of a person's life which leads him or her to seek help for drug dependency.

DEFENSE. A rationalization or justification of one's inappropriate conduct or behavior.

DELUSION. A false, irrational, and persistent belief.

DENIAL. A main component of drug dependency in which one is unwilling or unable to recognize a problem with alcohol and/or drugs. This is also frequently seen in codependents.

DEPENDENCE. *Psychological:* profound emotional need for continued use of a mind-altering drug. *Physical (addiction):* the compulsive need to use a drug to either get high and/or avoid withdrawal, despite adverse physical, financial, or legal consequences.

DETOXIFICATION. The process by which a drug-addicted person returns to normal physical and mental functioning. This may be accomplished by the abrupt end of drug use ("cold turkey"), or by gradual discontinuation of the drug under medical supervision.

DRUG. A medication or chemical introduced into the body for a specific effect.

DRY DRUNK. Attitudes and behaviors of the sober alcoholic or drug-dependent person that seem identical to attitudes and behaviors seen during periods of active drinking or drug use.

ENABLER. An individual who provides the means, or opportunity, for the alcoholic or drug-dependent person to continue drinking or drug use.

EXPLAINING. To minimize the significance of one's behavior by giving reasons or excuses for that behavior. A defense mechanism.

FEEDBACK. Information from others in which they give their perception of a person and how that person appears to them.

FLASHBACK(S). The recurrence of a previous drug-induced experience which occurs despite the absence of that drug due to psychological events in which the memory recreates the effect of the drug.

GENERALIZE. To make vague or indefinite statements in order to avoid reality or specific problems. A defense mechanism.

GROUP THERAPY. A form of treatment used with a number of individuals (at the same time) to stimulate positive change and personal growth.

GROWTH. Progressive development toward personal, emotional, and spiritual maturity.

GUILT. The feeling, either real or false, that one has violated a moral, social, or ethical (or biblical) principle.

HALLUCINATION. A visual, auditory, olfactory, or tactile perception that does not exist outside of one's mind.

INTERVENTION. A process of 1) giving factual information about one's alcohol and/or drug abuse, 2) presenting options to aid in dealing with one's addiction, and 3) informing of the consequences if treatment is refused.

MANIPULATION. The act of managing, influencing, or inducing another to do as one wishes, usually in a devious or dishonest manner.

MEDICAL DETOXIFICATION. The administration of medication for the purpose of managing withdrawal from drug addiction and prevention of complications.

MINIMIZING. Reducing to the smallest possible significance, extent, or degree. A defense mechanism.

NONVERBAL. The gestures, facial expressions, and body language by which one communicates thoughts, emotions, and feelings without using words.

NURTURE. To provide support and encouragement in order to enhance growth leading to drug-free living.

ORIENTED. The ability to distinguish person, place, time or situation; not confused.

PROJECTING. As a part of denial, and in order to avoid guilt and responsibility, the placing of blame for one's faults, mistakes, and behavior on others. A defense mechanism.

PUSHING BUTTONS. Knowing a person's sensitive emotional areas, and then deliberately saying or doing what will cause them to react.

RATIONALIZATION. A valid-sounding excuse to avoid responsibility for inappropriate and irresponsible behavior. A defense mechanism.

RECOVERY. The process of restoration and maintenance of physical, mental, emotional, and spiritual health after one stops using mind-altering drugs. This is a life-long process.

RECOVERING/SOBRIETY. Living without the use of mind-altering drugs, characterized by appropriate thinking, a productive lifestyle, and the use of healthy, nondrug coping mechanisms.

RELAPSE OR "SLIP." Self-prescribed use of *any* addicting drug by a recovering person. The term *slip* usually refers to a brief, short-lived relapse followed by a return to abstinence or active treatment.

RESENTMENT. A feeling of indignation, displeasure, or ill will at something or someone because of a perceived wrong, insult, or injury.

RIGID. Being fixed in opinion, belief, or behavior, and being unable and/or unwilling to consider or utilize alternatives.

ROLE PLAYING. A therapeutic group setting in which fellow patients become players, acting out another person's behavior for the purpose of giving insight and stimulating that person to change his or her behavior.

SABOTAGE. To destroy or undermine the treatment process.

SEIZURE. A disturbance to the nervous system which can manifest itself in convulsions, disturbances in sensation, alteration in perception, and loss of consciousness; sometimes it is associated with alcohol or drug withdrawal.

SELF-HELP GROUP. A group of people recovering from some form of drug addiction who agree to assist each other in the recovery process.

SOBER. May mean drug-free, clean, or straight. In AA there is a distinction between the terms *clean, straight, dry,* and *sober.* Clean or straight usually refer to abstinence from drugs other than alcohol. Dry describes a person who refrains from the use of alcohol but does not participate actively in the spiritual aspect of AA. Sober is reserved for alcoholics who work a program of recovery that includes the twelve steps and emphasizes spiritual values, positive thinking, and a productive lifestyle.

SOBRIETY. Being stable in one's emotional, physical, and spiritual life without using alcohol or other mind-altering drugs.

STAGES OF RECOVERY. The process by which a person becomes drug free. When referring to alcoholism and/or drug dependency, the stages are admission, compliance, acceptance, and surrender.

TOLERANCE. Physiological adaptation to psychoactive drugs so that a greater dose of a given drug is required to achieve euphoria.

TOUGH LOVE. Loving or caring for others enough to be confrontive and nonsupportive of their inappropriate behavior, and not protecting them from the consequences of that behavior.

TOXIC. Harmful, destructive, or deadly; poisonous—i.e., alcohol as a toxic drug.

TREATMENT/REHABILITATION. A process by which a drug-addicted person receives organized help with the goal of his/her eventual return to normal functioning. *Social Model of Treatment:* consists primarily of education and counseling. Psychoactive medications are not used, even for detoxification. *Medical Model:* medications, nursing care, and counseling are the basic elements of treatment traditionally carried out in hospitals, but used increasingly in outpatient care. *Psychiatric Model:* uses insight-oriented psychotherapy as a core element in treatment. Also assumes that drug use is a mental illness or is caused by it.

UNMANAGEABLE. Being unable to conduct or direct one's own life physically, emotionally, and spiritually.

VACILLATING. Shifting rapidly from one position or decision to another; wavering. A defense mechanism.

VERBALIZATION. The ability of an individual to express one's thoughts and feelings by the effective use of words.

VERBOSE. Talking excessively in order to avoid dealing with the problems at hand. A defense mechanism.

WARM FUZZIES/STROKES. The expression of a positive feeling toward another; a look, an embrace, or any other means that would show caring and support for another.

WITHDRAWAL/ABSTINENCE SYNDROME. The signs and symptoms following discontinuation of a drug upon which the user has become dependent.

DRUGS OF ABUSE: SLANG TERMS

A-BOMB. Marijuana and heroin mixed together and smoked.

ACAPULCO GOLD. An especially potent, high-quality marijuana grown near Acapulco, Mexico.

ACID. A slang term for LSD-25; from d-lysergic acid diethylamide tartrate.

ACID HEAD. A habitual heavy user of LSD.

ACID ROCK. A type of rock 'n' roll music using electronic sound which is associated with the use of hallucinogens, particularly LSD.

ANGEL DUST. Phencyclidine. In powder form, it is mixed with another hallucinogen, usually marijuana, and smoked, snorted, or taken orally.

BAD. A term for drugs that are considered very good and very potent.

BAD TRIP. A frightening reaction after the use of a hallucinogenic drug, which can cause a temporary or chronic psychosis.

BAG. A measurement of heroin (usually contains about five grains of diluted heroin, 1–5 percent pure) or marijuana (usually contains $1/7$–$1/5$ oz.). The term is also applied to a person who is using one drug exclusively: "He's in an LSD bag."

BALLOONS. Drugs (heroin or cocaine) are sometimes packaged for sale in balloons: if a sale is interrupted by police the balloon can be swallowed and later excreted; a method of concealing drugs also used in smuggling.

BANG. A narcotics injection, or the act of injecting a narcotic.

BASING. Using cocaine free base.

BENDER. Being on a drug spree. Used primarily in the case of alcohol, as in "on a bender."

BENNIES. Benzedrine (an amphetamine).

BIG BAGS. Five- and ten-dollar bags of heroin.

BIG MAN. The person who supplies a pusher with drugs.

BLACK BEAUTIES, BLACK MOLLIES. Biphetamine (an amphetamine).

BLACK TAR. A new form of heroin that is black and higher in potency.

BLACK RUSSIAN. Hashish (a potent form of marijuana).

BLOW YOUR MIND. To feel the effects of hallucinogens; also, to lose touch with reality and not have mental control.

BLUE ANGELS, BLUE DEVILS. Amytal Sodium (a barbiturate).

BOMB. A large-size marijuana cigarette; also, high-quality heroin which has been diluted very little.

BOMBED OUT. Feeling the effects of a drug.

BONG. A water pipe used to smoke marijuana. The smoke bubbles through the water and eliminates some of the harshness.

THE BOOK. The *Physicians' Desk Reference;* also called "the Bible."

BOOST. To shoplift, a common way for an addict to obtain money to support a habit.

BRICK. A pressed block of marijuana, opium, or morphine. In the case of marijuana, it weighs one pound.

BUMMER. A frightening reaction after taking a drug. A bum (or bad) trip.

BURN. Cheating or being cheated in drug deals.

BURNOUT, BURNED OUT. Refers (1) to a chronic drug user who is so weary of the hassle of obtaining drugs that drug habit stops, or (2) heavy marijuana smokers, particularly young people, who become dull and apathetic and withdraw from their usual activities. They are called "burnouts" by their peers.

BUZZ. Feeling the effects of a drug, usually alcohol or marijuana.

C. Cocaine.

CANDY. Drugs.

CANDY MAN. A person who sells drugs.

CENT. In drug language a cent refers to a dollar, a nickel is $5, a dime is $10.

CHASING THE DRAGON. Inhaling the fumes of heroin that has been mixed with barbiturate powder and melted over a flame.

CHINA WHITE. Heroin that is pure white and very potent.

CHIPPING. Using drugs irregularly and infrequently.

CHRISTMAS TREES. Dexamyl (an amphetamine).

CHUG-A-LUG. To consume an alcoholic beverage, particularly beer, without pausing to breathe between swallows. The practice is common among teenagers and college students who hold chug-a-lug contests. These contests can be extremely dangerous because aside from producing rapid intoxication, the practice can result in coma or death, especially when hard liquor is being consumed.

CLEAN. Not using or possessing drugs.

COAST. To experience the drowsy, somnolent effects of heroin.

COKE. Cocaine.

COKE HEAD. A heavy user of cocaine.

COKE "WHORE." A person who will do anything to get cocaine.

COLD TURKEY. The act of being taken off a drug suddenly and completely, without any preparation; also, quitting a drug without the benefit of medication.

COME (COMING) DOWN. Returning to a normal state after drug effects have worn off. For heroin addicts this state signals the beginning of withdrawal symptoms.

COOK. Heating heroin powder with water until it dissolves and is ready for injection.

COP. The act of purchasing a drug.

CRACK. Crystalline cocaine that is burned and the fumes inhaled. It is highly addicting.

CRANK. Amphetamines.

CRASH. Suddenly falling asleep after the heavy use of stimulants or to return to a normal state when the drug effects have worn off.

CRYSTAL. Amphetamines that are soluble for injection, so-called because they are supplied in the form of white crystal.

DEAL, DEALING. To sell drugs, particularly narcotics.

DEALER. A person who sells drugs, particularly narcotics.

DEXIES. Dexedrine, Dexamyl (amphetamines).

DIRTY. Having drugs in one's possession (opposite of "clean").

DOPE. Narcotic drugs.

DOPE FIEND. A person who uses dope.

DOWN, DOWNER, DOWNIE. A slang term for barbiturates. An amphetamine user often takes a tranquilizer to reverse the stimulant effects of amphetamines when they become too intense.

DRIED OUT. Detoxified from a drug.

DRUGGIES. People who frequently experiment with a wide variety of drugs; also, high school/college youth who use drugs regularly.

187

EIGHT BALL. Approximately three grams of cocaine.

FACTORY. A secret place where drugs are diluted, packaged, or otherwise prepared for sale.

FIX. The injecting of heroin or the heroin itself (also applies to using any drug intravenously).

FLASHING. A term applied to sniffing glue.

FLOATING. Being under the effects of a drug.

FOOTBALLS. Dilaudid.

FREAK OUT. A bad, panicky reaction to a drug; or simply to take a drug.

FRONT. To sell drugs to another person on credit.

FRUIT SALAD. A game, usually played by teenagers, in which one pill is swallowed from each bottle in a medicine cabinet.

GANGA, GANJA. Extremely potent marijuana grown in Jamaica.

GARBAGE HEAD. A person who will use any drug available to get high.

GET OFF. To experience the effects of a drug; also, to take a heroin injection.

GETTING ON. To feel the effects of marijuana.

GLOW. To feel the euphoric effects of a drug.

GOLD DUST. Cocaine.

GOOFBALL. Barbiturates and amphetamines.

GRASS. Marijuana.

GROWER. A person who grows marijuana but does not get involved in its distribution or smuggling.

H. Heroin.

HEAD. A person who favors a particular drug, as in pot head.

HIT. To take a drug, particularly heroin or marijuana.

HOOKED. Addicted to a drug.

HORSE. Heroin.

JANE. Marijuana.

JOINT. A marijuana cigarette.

JUNK. Drugs, particularly heroin.

JUNKIE. A heroin addict.

KICK, KICKING. To break a drug addiction, as in "kicking the habit."

KILLER WEED. High-potency marijuana, or marijuana that is mixed with phencyclidine.

KNOCKOUT DROPS. A mixture of alcohol and chloral hydrate that causes a person to lose consciousness.

LADY, LADY SNOW. Cocaine.

LID. A measurement of weight used for marijuana. Ranging from 3/4 to 1 ounce, it is enough for approximately 40 marijuana cigarettes.

LIGHT UP. To smoke marijuana.

LOADED. To be heavily intoxicated, whether from alcohol or any other drug.

MARY ANN, MARY JANE, MARY WARNER, MARY WEAVER. Marijuana.

METH. Methamphetamine, Methedrine (amphetamines).

MEXICAN BROWN. Marijuana grown in Mexico that has a higher resin content than "Mexican Green." It is also a slang term for brown heroin.

M. J.. Marijuana, an abbreviation for Mary Jane.

MONKEY, MONKEY ON (MY) BACK. A person's drug dependence or habit.

NARC, NARCO. A narcotics police officer.

NEEDLE HABIT. Some addicts, often referred to as "needle freaks," are not particular about what drug they inject but get their thrills simply from the act of injecting.

NICKEL BAG. A package, usually of marijuana or heroin, which is worth $5.

NOD, NODDING. To feel the initial effects of a heroin injection—pleasurable drowsiness and peacefulness—probably so called because the head nods forward.

NOSE CANDY. Cocaine.

O.D. Overdose.

PANIC. Anxiety (1) resulting from an addict's shortage of drugs or inability to buy them, or (2) due to the drug itself, particularly cocaine.

PAPERS. (1) Folded pieces of paper, or packages containing narcotics, particularly heroin, or (2) cigarette paper used to make marijuana cigarettes.

PARAPHERNALIA. The equipment needed to inject heroin, smoke pot, or freebase cocaine.

PEP PILLS. Amphetamines.

PILL HEAD. A person who frequently uses amphetamines and barbiturates or is addicted to prescription drugs.

PINK LADIES. Barbiturates.

POP, POPPING. To take a pill; also, the subcutaneous injection of heroin.

POPPERS. Amyl nitrite (an inhalant) in small glass vials that are broken and from which the chemical is inhaled.

POT. Marijuana.

POT HEAD. A heavy user of marijuana.

PUSHER. A dealer who sells drugs directly to an addict; a person who is one step below the wholesaler in the drug distribution system.

Q's. Quaaludes (a sleeping pill).

RED AND BLUES. Tuinal (barbiturates).

RED BIRDS, RED BULLETS, RED DEVILS, RED DOLLS, REDS. Seconal (from the color), a barbiturate.

REEFER. Marijuana.

RIG. Apparatus for injecting heroin or smoking pot.

RIPPED. To be highly intoxicated by a drug.

ROACH. A marijuana cigarette when it has burned down too far to be held with the fingers (at which point it looks like a cockroach).

ROACH CLIP. An instrument (pin, tweezers, etc.) used to hold a roach.

ROCK. Cocaine in chunk form, usually more potent.

RUN. A period of heavy and prolonged use of a particular drug, usually referring to amphetamines or cocaine.

RUSH. The initial euphoric effects after a heroin or amphetamine injection.

SCORE. To buy a drug.

SCRIPT. A prescription for a narcotic; an abbreviation of the word *prescription.*

SHOOTING GALLERY. A location where addicts inject heroin.

SHOOT UP. To inject a drug, particularly heroin.

SICK. To experience the beginning of withdrawal symptoms.

SMACK. Heroin.

SNOW. Cocaine.

SPEED. Amphetamines, particularly Methedrine.

SPEEDBALL. A mixture of heroin and cocaine, or heroin and amphetamine, which is injected.

SPEED FREAK. A heavy user of amphetamines.

SPOON. A measurement of heroin ($1/16$ of an ounce), or cocaine ($1/4$ of a teaspoon).

STASH. A cache of hidden drugs.

STONED. Being high on a drug.

STP. An hallucinogen. (Probably from the brand-name motor oil additive that promises increased power.)

STRAIGHT. A person who doesn't use drugs, a square; also a term for a regular cigarette.

STRUNG OUT. An addict who has a severe habit; or an addict's physical appearance because of a severe habit.

TEETOTAL, TEETOTALER. Total abstinence from alcohol, or one who totally abstains.

TEXAS TEA. Marijuana.

TIGHT. A person who is intoxicated by alcohol or other drugs.

TOKE. To smoke a marijuana cigarette. The term refers to both smoking the whole cigarette and just taking a puff.

TOKE PIPES. Pipes used to smoke marijuana.

TOKE UP. To light a marijuana cigarette.

TOOT. To snort or sniff cocaine, as in "let's have a toot."

TRIP. The act of taking a hallucinogen, particularly LSD; or the effects of its ingestion.

TURN ON. To take a drug or encourage another to do so; to feel the effects of a drug.

UPPER, UPPERS. Amphetamines.

USER. A person who uses drugs.

WASTED. To lose consciousness from drug intoxication.

WEED. Marijuana.

WHITE LADY. Cocaine, heroin.

WIPED OUT. Acute drug intoxication.

WIRED. A person who is feeling the high effects of amphetamines. The terms also applies to a heroin addict.

ZONKED. Acutely intoxicated by a drug.

APPENDIX 3

RESOURCES

Organizations

The following organizations provide educational materials about drug abuse, its prevention, and its treatment. Many of them also provide support for the families of drug and alcohol users.

The National Federation of Parents for Drug-Free Youth (NFP)
1820 Franwall Avenue, Suite 16
Silver Spring, MD 20902
800-554-KIDS

NFP is the leading parents' organization in the country and has chapters or affiliates in many communities. They provide support, guidance, and information for parent groups.

Parent Resource Institute for Drug Education (PRIDE)
Georgia State University
University Plaza
Physical Education Building, Room 137
Atlanta, GA 30303
800-241-9746

PRIDE is the leading support group for the parents' networking movement. It can help set up programs to establish a drug-free school environment.

The American Council for Drug Education (ACDE)
5820 Hubbard Drive
Rockville, MD 20852
301-294-0600

National Clearinghouse for Drug Abuse Information
The National Institute on Drug Abuse (NIDA)
Room 10A56, Parklawn Building
5600 Fishers Lane
Rockville, MD 20857
301-443-6500

National Clearinghouse for Alcohol Information
National Institute on Alcohol Abuse and Alcoholism
1776 East Jefferson Street
Fourth Floor
Rockville, MD 20852
301-468-2600

Alcoholics Anonymous World Services, Inc. (AA)
Box 459
Grand Central Station
New York, NY 10163

Addiction Research Foundation
33 Russell Street
Toronto, Canada
416-595-6056

Narcotics Anonymous World Services Office, Inc. (NA)
P. O. Box 622
Sun Valley, CA 91352
818-780-3951

National Association for Children of Alcoholics (NCOA)
31706 Coast Highway, Suite 201
South Laguna, CA 92677
714-499-3889

Nonprofit organization that functions as a clearinghouse and network for (adult) children of alcoholics. Publishes a quarterly newsletter, holds regional and national conferences, and publishes books and pamphlets on children of alcoholics.

193

Johnson Institute
510 First Avenue, North
Minneapolis, MN 55403-1607
800-231-5165

Hazelden (Foundation) Educational Materials
Pleasant Valley Road
Box 176
Center City, MN 55012-0176
800-328-9000

Both the Johnson Institute and Hazelden Foundation provide educational materials for schools, businesses, and families about drug abuse and its treatment. They both offer treatment programs in the Minneapolis area.

TOUGHLOVE
P. O. Box 1069
Doylestown, PA 18901
215-348-7090

A national self-help group for parents, children, and communities emphasizing cooperation, personal initiative, avoidance of blame, and action.

Families in Action
3845 N. Druid Hills Road, Suite 300
Decatur, GA 30033
404-325-5799

Maintains a drug information center with more than 100,000 documents. Publishes *Drug Abuse Update*, a newsletter.

In Great Britain

Narcotics Anonymous
Box 246
London SW10
Telephone: 01-871-0505

The Institute for the Study of Drug Dependence
1-Y Hatton Place
Hatton Garden
London EC1N 8ND

The Teachers Advisory Council on Alcohol and Drug Education
2 Mount Street
Manchester M2 SN9

Books

Professional

Bratter, Thomas E., and Forrest, Gary G. *Alcoholism and Substance Abuse*. New York: The Free Press, 1985.

Gorski, Terence T., and Miller, Merlene. *Staying Sober*, A Guide for Relapse Prevention. Independence, Mo.: Independence Press, 1986.

Johnson Institute Books. *How to Use Intervention in Your Professional Practice*. Minneapolis: Johnson Institute, 1987.

Johnson, Vernon E. *I'll Quit Tomorrow*. New York: Harper & Row, 1980. A classic in the field of alcoholic treatment.

McKim, William A. *Drugs and Behavior*, An Introduction to Behavioral Pharmacology. Englewood Cliffs, N.J.: Prentice-Hall, 1986.

General

DuPont, Jr., Robert L., M.D. *Getting Tough on Gateway Drugs*. Washington, D.C.: American Psychiatric Press, 1984.

Macdonald, Donald Ian, M.D. *Drugs, Drinking and Adolescents*. Chicago: Year Book Medical Publishers, 1984. Dr. Macdonald shares his own adolescent's battle with drugs. He is now the head of Alcohol, Drug Abuse, and Mental Health Administration.

Manatt, Marsha, Ph.D. *Parents, Peers and Pot II:* Parents in Action. Rockville, Md.: National Institute on Drug Abuse, 1983. Written by one of the founders of the parents' peer network movement. Will help anyone organize the parents in a community.

Mann, Peggy. *Pot Safari*. New York: Woodmere Press, 1985. Latest research into the hazards of marijuana. Scientifically confronts the notion that pot is a safe drug.

Perkins, William and Nancy. *Raising Drug-Free Kids in a Drug-Filled World*. New York: Harper & Row, 1986.

Polson, Beth, and Newton, Miller. *Not My Kid*. New York: Avon, 1984. A 224-page guide for parents to aid in prevention, recognition, and treatment of adolescent chemical use. It is especially strong on overcoming denial and recognizing problems, with numerous personal vignettes.

Rosellini, Gayle, and Worden, Mark. *Of Course You're Angry.* San Francisco: Harper & Row, 1985. One of the best discussions about anger and how to deal with it; worthwhile for anyone who has a problem with anger.

Spickard, Anderson, M.D., and Thompson, Barbara R. *Dying for a Drink.* Waco, Tex.: Word, 1985. This book deals with both the medical and spiritual aspects of alcoholism and recovery from it. Dr. Spickard heads the alcoholism treatment program at Vanderbilt University.

Tobias, Joyce. *Kids and Drugs:* A Handbook for Parents and Professionals. Annandale, Va.: Panda Press, 1986. A handbook about adolescent drug and alcohol use, the effects of drugs and the drug culture, stages of chemical use, parent groups and their creation and maintenance, and resources available to parents and professionals.

Schools Without Drugs. Washington, D.C.: U.S. Department of Education, 1986. Provides specific guidelines for establishing a drug-free environment for our children. Very practical. Copy available by phoning 1-800-624-0100, or by writing Schools Without Drugs, Pueblo, CO 81009.

Woititz, Janet G. *Adult Children of Alcoholics.* Pompano Beach, Fla.: Health Communications, Inc., 1983.

York, Phyllis and David, and Wachtel, Ted. *Toughlove.* Garden City, N.Y.: Doubleday, 1982. The Yorks founded the Toughlove movement which has chapters in most major cities. Toughlove helps parents band together to control their unruly teens.

Christian Drug Treatment Programs

The following is a list of programs which have a Christian emphasis in their treatment of drug addiction. It is not comprehensive, but these programs are personally known by the authors.

Inpatient

Care Unit Hospital
Christian Therapy Program
401 South Tustin Avenue
Orange, CA 92666
(714) 633-9582

Garland Memorial Hospital
2300 Marie Curie
Garland, TX 75042
(214) 276-9511

Rapha
Box 580355
Houston, TX 77258
(713) 472-2657

Vanderbilt Institute for Treatment of Alcoholism
Vanderbilt University Medical Center
Nashville, TN 37232
(615) 322-6158

Outpatient

La Canada Presbyterian Church
626 Foothill Blvd.
La Canada, CA 91011
(213) 790-6708

Sponsors a program called THE ELEVENTH STEP, which offers Christ-centered fellowship for those recovering from drug and alcohol addiction. They have materials prepared to assist other churches in establishing their own ministry.

Transforming Others Under Christ's Hand (TOUCH)
1226 S. Presa
San Antonio, TX 78210
(512) 534-6116

TOUCH is an outpatient program that offers medical treatment along with biblical counseling for heroin and other narcotic addicts.

Community Health Resources
13409 N.W. Military Hwy.
Suite 310
San Antonio, TX 78231
(512) 493-3291

Provides outpatient evaluation and treatment of chemical dependency and the related problems such as codependency. Offers diagnosis, screening, treatment, and counseling services. Staff believes that the whole person—body, mind, and spirit—must be treated if one is to break free from the bonds of addiction.

Residential Programs

His Mansion
Box 40
Hillsboro, NH 03244-0040
(603) 464-5555

Teen Challenge
P. O. Box 198
Rehrersburg, PA 19550
(717) 933-4181

Both of these programs offer a one-year program that provides for drug-free living, personal counseling, Bible study, and vocational training.

SIGNS OF TEENAGE DRUG ABUSE

Change in Behavior

- Chronic lying, stealing, cheating, secretiveness
- Changes in friends, unwillingness to bring them home or talk about them
- Severe mood swings
- Unpredictable and inappropriate behavior (anger, irritability, hostility)
- Loss of interest in hobbies and extracurricular activities
- Lack of motivation and self-discipline
- Withdrawal from usual family activities
- Unexplained loss of money and possessions, or—
- Unexplained possession of large amounts of money
- Items of value missing from the house
- Frequent unexplained absences from home, never home on time

Change in School Performance

- Grades markedly below previous levels
- Assignments not completed
- Frequent absences and discipline problems

Change in Friends, Music, and Activities

- New friends appear to be druggies
- Frequent listening to "heavy metal" or "acid rock"

- Conversation is preoccupied with drugs
- Drug-related slogans on clothing

Deterioration of Health

- Unkempt appearance, poor personal hygiene
- Poor attention span, difficulty in concentration
- Frequent respiratory illnesses
- Dilated pupils, chronically bloodshot eyes, slurred speech
- Poor physical coordination, incoherent thinking

Drug Use Signs and Paraphernalia

- Possession of water pipes, rolling papers, small decongestant bottles, small butane torches, "roach" clips, stash cans
- Possession of drugs or evidence of drugs
- Presence of butts, seeds, or leaves in clothing or around house
- Odor of drugs, use of incense, or frequent use of "cover-up" scents

APPENDIX 5

MICHIGAN ALCOHOLISM SCREENING TEST

The following questions will help you assess whether a counselee or someone else you know has a problem with alcohol. If the score (as determined below) is greater than 4 the individual should seek evaluation and treatment.

1. Do you feel you are a normal drinker? (By normal we mean you drink less than or as much as most other people.)
2. Have you ever awakened the morning after some drinking the night before and found that you could not remember a part of the evening?
3. Does your wife, husband, a parent or other near relative ever worry or complain about your drinking?
4. Can you stop drinking without a struggle after one or two drinks?
5. Do you ever feel guilty about your drinking?
6. Do friends or relatives think you are a normal drinker?
7. Are you able to stop drinking when you want to?
8. Have you ever attended a meeting of Alcoholics Anonymous?
9. Have you ever been in physical fights when drinking?
10. Has drinking ever created problems between you and your wife, husband, a parent or other near relative?
11. Has your wife, husband, a parent or other near relative ever gone to anyone for help about your drinking?

12. Have you ever lost friends because of your drinking?
13. Have you ever been in trouble at work because of your drinking?
14. Have you ever lost a job because of drinking?
15. Have you ever neglected your obligations, your family or work for two or more days in a row because you were drinking?
16. Do you drink before noon fairly often?
17. Have you ever been told you have liver trouble (Cirrhosis)?
18. After heavy drinking have you ever had delirium tremens (DT's), severe shaking or seen or heard things that weren't really there?
19. Have you ever gone to anyone for help about your drinking?
20. Have you ever been in a hospital because of drinking?
21. Have you ever been a patient in a psychiatric hospital or on a psychiatric ward of a general hospital where drinking was part of the problem that resulted in hospitalization?
22. Have you ever been seen at a psychiatric or mental health clinic or gone to any doctor, social worker or clergyman for help with any emotional problem where drinking was part of the problem?
23. Have you ever been arrested for drunk driving under the influence of alcoholic beverages?
24. Have you ever been arrested, even for a few hours, because of other drunken behavior?

Scoring Key

1. Yes 0, No 2	9. Yes 1, No 0	17. Yes 2, No 0
2. Yes 2, No 0	10. Yes 2, No 0	18. Yes 2, No 0
3. Yes 1, No 0	11. Yes 2, No 0	19. Yes 5, No 0
4. Yes 0, No 2	12. Yes 2, No 0	20. Yes 5, No 0
5. Yes 1, No 0	13. Yes 2, No 0	21. Yes 2, No 0
6. Yes 0, No 2	14. Yes 2, No 0	22. Yes 2, No 0
7. Yes 0, No 2	15. Yes 2, No 0	23. Yes 2, No 0
8. Yes 5, No 0	16. Yes 1, No 0	24. Yes 2, No 0

Interpretation

Score	Degree of Alcoholism
0–4	nonalcoholic
5–6	suggestive of alcoholism
7 or more	definite alcoholism

Positive response to #8, 19, or 20 considered diagnostic of alcoholism.

APPENDIX 6

DRUG ABUSE SCREENING TEST

The following questions refer only to the use of drugs other than alcohol. These include: over-the-counter and prescription drugs, and the drugs of abuse, such as cocaine and marijuana. Source: Johns Hopkins University.

1. Have you used drugs other than those required for medical reasons?
2. Have you abused prescription drugs?
3. Do you abuse more than one drug at a time?
4. Can you get through the week without using drugs?
5. Are you always able to stop using drugs when you want to?
6. Have you had "blackouts" or "flashbacks" as a result of drug use?
7. Do you ever feel bad or guilty about your drug use?
8. Does your spouse (or parents) ever complain about your involvement with drugs?
9. Has drug abuse created problems between you and your spouse or your parents?
10. Have you lost friends because of your use of drugs?
11. Have you neglected your family because of your use of drugs?
12. Have you been in trouble at work because of drug abuse?
13. Have you lost a job because of drug abuse?
14. Have you gotten into fights when under the influence of drugs?
15. Have you engaged in illegal activities in order to obtain drugs?

16. Have you been arrested for possession of illegal drugs?
17. Have you ever experienced withdrawal symptoms (felt sick) when you stopped taking drugs?
18. Have you had medical problems as a result of your drug use (e.g., memory loss, hepatitis, convulsions, bleeding, etc.)?
19. Have you gone to anyone for help for a drug problem?
20. Have you been involved in a treatment program especially related to drug use?

Scoring Key

Score one point for each Yes answer, on #1–3, 6–20; score one point for each No answer on #4 and 5.

Interpretation

Score	Degree of Drug Abuse Problem
0	none
1–5	low level
6–10	moderate level
11–15	substantial level
16–20	severe level

A low score does not necessarily mean that a person is free of drug-related problems. Any positive response may mean that you or someone you know needs help.

A Chart of Alcohol Addiction and Recovery (Jellinek)

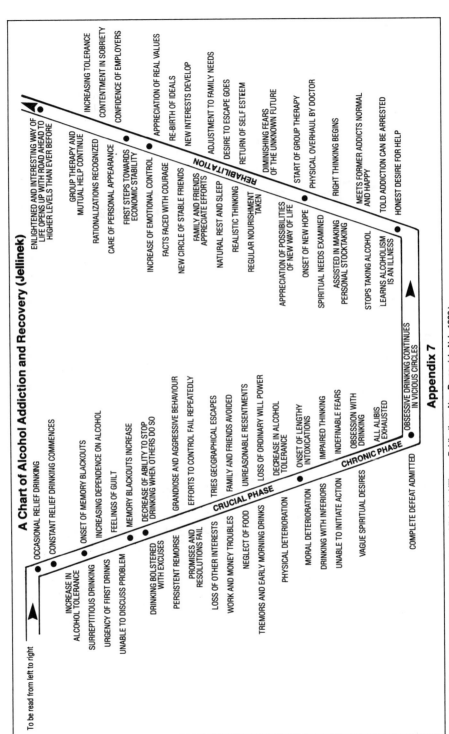

To be read from left to right

INCREASE IN ALCOHOL TOLERANCE
SURREPTITIOUS DRINKING
URGENCY OF FIRST DRINKS
UNABLE TO DISCUSS PROBLEM

OCCASIONAL RELIEF DRINKING
CONSTANT RELIEF DRINKING COMMENCES
ONSET OF MEMORY BLACKOUTS
INCREASING DEPENDENCE ON ALCOHOL
FEELINGS OF GUILT
MEMORY BLACKOUTS INCREASE
DECREASE OF ABILITY TO STOP DRINKING WHEN OTHERS DO SO

DRINKING BOLSTERED WITH EXCUSES
PERSISTENT REMORSE
PROMISES AND RESOLUTIONS FAIL
LOSS OF OTHER INTERESTS
WORK AND MONEY TROUBLES
NEGLECT OF FOOD
TREMORS AND EARLY MORNING DRINKS

GRANDIOSE AND AGGRESSIVE BEHAVIOUR
EFFORTS TO CONTROL FAIL REPEATEDLY
TRIES GEOGRAPHICAL ESCAPES
FAMILY AND FRIENDS AVOIDED
UNREASONABLE RESENTMENTS
LOSS OF ORDINARY WILL POWER
DECREASE IN ALCOHOL TOLERANCE

PHYSICAL DETERIORATION
ONSET OF LENGTHY INTOXICATIONS
MORAL DETERIORATION
IMPAIRED THINKING
DRINKING WITH INFERIORS
UNABLE TO INITIATE ACTION
INDEFINABLE FEARS
OBSESSION WITH DRINKING
VAGUE SPIRITUAL DESIRES
ALL ALIBIS EXHAUSTED

COMPLETE DEFEAT ADMITTED

OBSESSIVE DRINKING CONTINUES IN VICIOUS CIRCLES

CRUCIAL PHASE

CHRONIC PHASE

ENLIGHTENED AND INTERESTING WAY OF LIFE OPENS UP WITH ROAD AHEAD TO HIGHER LEVELS THAN EVER BEFORE
INCREASING TOLERANCE
CONTENTMENT IN SOBRIETY
CONFIDENCE OF EMPLOYERS
GROUP THERAPY AND MUTUAL HELP CONTINUE
RATIONALIZATIONS RECOGNIZED
CARE OF PERSONAL APPEARANCE
APPRECIATION OF REAL VALUES
RE-BIRTH OF IDEALS
NEW INTERESTS DEVELOP
ADJUSTMENT TO FAMILY NEEDS
DESIRE TO ESCAPE GOES
RETURN OF SELF ESTEEM

FIRST STEPS TOWARDS ECONOMIC STABILITY
INCREASE OF EMOTIONAL CONTROL
FACTS FACED WITH COURAGE
NEW CIRCLE OF STABLE FRIENDS
FAMILY AND FRIENDS APPRECIATE EFFORTS
NATURAL REST AND SLEEP
REALISTIC THINKING
REGULAR NOURISHMENT TAKEN

DIMINISHING FEARS OF THE UNKNOWN FUTURE
START OF GROUP THERAPY
PHYSICAL OVERHAUL BY DOCTOR
RIGHT THINKING BEGINS
MEETS FORMER ADDICTS NORMAL AND HAPPY
TOLD ADDICTION CAN BE ARRESTED
HONEST DESIRE FOR HELP

APPRECIATION OF POSSIBILITIES OF NEW WAY OF LIFE
ONSET OF NEW HOPE
SPIRITUAL NEEDS EXAMINED
ASSISTED IN MAKING PERSONAL STOCKTAKING
STOPS TAKING ALCOHOL
LEARNS ALCOHOLISM IS AN ILLNESS

REHABILITATION

Appendix 7

(From Jellinek, E., *The Disease Concept of Alcoholism*, published by Hillhouse Publications, New Brunswick, N.J., 1960.)

The Progression and Recovery of the FAMILY in the Disease of Alcoholism

The progression and recovery symptoms listed are based on the *most repeated experiences* of family members in the disease of alcoholism or other chemical dependencies. While every symptom in the chart does not occur in every member of every family, or in the same sequence, it does portray an average chain reaction. The entire process may take years or it may occur in a very short time.

Without Help

Arguments
Distrust
Unhappiness
Religious Needs
Denial (fantasy)
Threats Made and Not Carried Through
Takes Responsibility
Loss of Interest
Imaginary Illnesses
Facade
Uses Prescribed Drugs
Loss of Self-Respect
Remorse
Social Withdrawal
Patent Medicine Use
Indefinable Fears
Drug Abuser
Bankruptcy of Alibis
Admits Defeat
Chronic Depression
Suicide Attempts

Blues
Intolerance
Suspicion
Problems Multiplying
Worry
Irritability
Seeks Help
Avoiding Reference
Extravagance
Self-Defense
Depression
Irrational Behavior
Self-Neglect
Alibi
Dishonesty
Infidelity
Isolation
Blames Others
Escape
Jealousy

Bottom

With Help

Awareness
Hope
Sincere Desire for Help
Recognizes Disease
Acceptance
Seeks Help
Recognition of Role
Need to Control Lessens
Shares with Others
Becomes Willing to Change
Cover Up Ceases
Begins to Relax
Developing Optimism
Daily Living Pattern Changes (Rest, Diet, Sleep)
Diminishing Fears
Return of Self-Esteem
Guilt is Gone
New Interests Develop
Return of Confidence
Appreciates Spiritual Values
Return of Respect of Family and Friends
Happiness
At Ease with Life

Honesty
Trust, Openness
Release
Spiritual Examination
New Friends
Service
Peace of Mind
Makes Amends
Love
Courage
Joy

Enlightened, Future Bright, Motivated to Higher Levels than Ever Believed Possible

Appendix 8

NOTES

Chapter 1. Nobody Starts Out to Be an Addict

1. "Suicide Note Warns Youths of 'White Lady of Death,'" *San Antonio Express-News*, April 29, 1982.

2. Peter Kerr, "Anatomy of an Issue: Drugs, the Evidence, the Reaction," *The New York Times*, November 17, 1986.

3. "Bubba: No More Beer Commercials," *San Antonio Express-News*, September 18, 1986.

4. "Seattle's Gene Anderson Throws the Book at White-Collar Coke Users Who Once Knew No Fear," *People*, February 2, 1987.

5. "Cocaine Addiction," *Postgraduate Medicine*, October 1986, 52.

6. John Gardner, *Spin the Bottle: The Autobiography of an Alcoholic* (London: F. Muller, 1964).

7. Vernon E. Johnson, *I'll Quit Tomorrow* (New York: Harper & Row, 1980), 8–47.

8. Mary Ellen Pinkham, "The Queen of Household Hints Comes Clean About a Problem that Nearly Ruined Her Life—Alcoholism," *People*, September 29, 1986, 110.

9. Thomas E. Bratter and Gary G. Forrest, *Alcoholism and Substance Abuse* (New York: The Free Press, 1985), 230.

10. The counselor may find additional help in two other volumes in the Resources for Christian Counseling series: *Counseling Those*

with Eating Disorders, vol. 4, by Raymond E. Vath, M.D., and *Counseling for Problems of Self-Control,* vol. 11, by Richard P. Walters, Ph.D.

Chapter 2. What You Don't Know Could Kill You

1. "Boy's Cocaine Death Shadows Town in Fear," *Dallas Times-Herald,* September 25, 1986.
2. "Road Back from Substance Abuse Especially Long, Hard for Athletes," *Journal of the American Medical Association,* November 21, 1986, 2645.
3. R. P. Donahue, et. al., "Alcohol and Hemorrhagic Stroke: The Honolulu Heart Program," *Journal of the American Medical Association,* May 2, 1986, 2311–14.
4. Robert L. DuPont, Jr., M.D., *Getting Tough on Gateway Drugs* (Washington, D.C.: American Psychiatric Press, 1984), 113.
5. *Working Paper: Projections of Alcohol Abusers, 1980, 1985, 1990* (Rockville, Md.: National Institute on Drug Abuse, 1985).
6. Lloyd D. Johnston, Patrick M. O'Malley, and Jerald G. Bachman, *Drug Use Among American High School Students, College Students, and Other Young Adults* (Rockville, Md.: National Institute on Drug Abuse, 1986), 52.
7. David E. Smith, "Cocaine-Alcohol Abuse: Epidemiological, Diagnostic and Treatment Considerations," *Journal of Psychoactive Drugs* 18 (April-June 1986): 120.
8. William A. McKim, *Drugs and Behavior,* An Introduction to Behavioral Pharmacology (Englewood Cliffs, N.J.: Prentice-Hall, 1986), 156.
9. DuPont, 32.

Chapter 3. The Equal Opportunity Destroyer

1. James Mills, *The Underground Empire* (Garden City, N.Y.: Doubleday, 1986), 3.
2. Ibid., 3.
3. "Rural Scourge: Once Mostly in Cities, Drugs Now Are Rife in Small Towns of U.S.," *Wall Street Journal,* September 23, 1986.
4. Ronald Kotulak, "The Struggle to Hang 'Keep Out' Sign on Gate to Drugs," *The Chicago Tribune,* December 28, 1986.
5. *The Underground Empire,* 1161.

6. "Seattle's Gene Anderson," *People.*

7. "The Marketplace—Illicit Drugs in Canada," *The Journal of the Addiction Research Foundation* 16:4 (April 1987), 16.

8. "Rural Scourge," *Wall Street Journal.*

9. Robert O'Brien and Sydney Cohen, *The Encyclopedia of Drug Abuse* (New York: Facts on File, 1984).

10. Data presented at the North American Conference on Cocaine Abuse and Its Treatment, September 16, 1987.

11. Johnston, O'Malley, and Bachman, 13–20.

12. DuPont, 62–64.

13. "Drug Abuse Hikes Cost of Insurance," *American Medical News*, October 10, 1986.

14. DuPont, 64.

Chapter 4. If Drugs Are So Bad, Why Do People Keep Using Them?

1. "Diary of a Teenage Drug User," *The Washington Post*, March 28, 1982.

2. "Warren McVea Receives Probated Sentence, Fine," *The Houston Post*, February 7, 1987.

3. McKim, 50.

4. C. S. Lewis, *Mere Christianity* (New York: Macmillan, 1960), 70.

Chapter 5. Helping Is Not Helping

1. Ann Landers, *San Antonio Express-News*, November 20, 1982.

2. C. S. Lewis, *The Problem of Pain* (New York: Macmillan, 1962), 93.

3. Anderson Spickard, M.D., and Barbara R. Thompson, *Dying for a Drink* (Waco, Tex.: Word Books, 1985), 64–66.

Chapter 6. Addiction Is a Family Affair

1. "Getting Tough with Teens," *Time*, June 8, 1981.

2. "Drug Test Results in Family Peace," *San Antonio Light*, December 30, 1986.

3. Janet G. Woititz, *Adult Children of Alcoholics* (Pompano Beach, Fla.: Health Communications, Inc., 1983), 55–86.

4. Sharon Wegscheider, *Another Chance* (Palo Alto, Calif.: Science and Behavior Books, Inc., 1981), 86.

Chapter 7. The Road to Recovery

1. Ann Landers, *San Antonio Express-News*, November 12, 1986.

2. Ibid.

3. *Alcoholics Anonymous*, 3rd ed. (New York: Alcoholics Anonymous World Services, Inc., 1976), 13.

4. Spickard and Thompson, 143–44.

Chapter 8. Picking Up the Pieces

1. Timmen L. Cermak, *Diagnosing and Treating Co-Dependence:* A Guide for Professionals Who Work with Chemical Dependents, Their Spouses and Children (Minneapolis: Johnson Institute, 1986), 1.

2. Robert Subby, *Lost in the Shuffle*, The Co-Dependent Reality (Pompano Beach, Fla.: Health Communications, Inc., 1987), 10, 11.

3. Elisabeth Kübler-Ross, *On Death and Dying* (New York: Macmillan, 1969).

4. Gayle Rosellini and Mark Worden, *Of Course You're Angry* (San Francisco: Harper & Row, 1985).

5. Philip Yancey, *Where Is God When It Hurts?* (Grand Rapids: Zondervan, 1977), 95–97.

6. Johnson, 120, 121.

7. Rosellini and Worden, 50, 51.

8. Ibid., 74.

9. Claudia Black, *It Will Never Happen to Me!* (Denver: M.A.C. Printing and Publications, 1981), 33–49.

10. Sharon Wegscheider-Cruse, *Choice-Making* (Pompano Beach, Fla.: Health Communications, Inc., 1985), 95, 96.

11. Wegscheider, *Another Chance*, 170–73.

Chapter 9. What Really Works in Treatment

1. Letter to the staff of TOUCH Drug Rehabilitation Program in San Antonio, Texas, June 1986.

2. Jerry Spicer and Patricia Owen, *Finding the Bottom Line*: The Cost-Impact of Employee Assistance and Chemical Dependency Treatment Programs (Minneapolis: Hazelden, 1985), 45.

Chapter 10. Working with Substance-Abuse Families

1. Edward Kaufman, "The Family of the Alcoholic Patient," *Psychomatics* 27:5 (May 1986), 352.
2. Cermak, 3.
3. William Springborn, *Foundations of Recovery* (Minneapolis: Hazelden Foundation, 1977.)
4. "NFL Medical Adviser Fights Relentlessly Against Drugs," *American Medical News*, October 24, 1986.
5. Brian Freemantle, *The Fix* (New York: TOR Books, 1986), 313.
6. Op. cit. *American Medical News.*
7. Shirley Dobson and Gloria Gaither, *Let's Make a Memory* (Waco, Tex.: Word Books, 1983).
8. "Kids Have Trouble With 'No' on Drugs," *The Denver Post*, December 26, 1986.

Chapter 11. Questions and Answers About Drug Use

1. "Coffee Consumption and Cholesterol," *Internal Medicine Alert* 5:12 (June 27, 1983), 45.
2. McKim, 85.
3. DuPont, 27.

INDEX

Tranxene, 43
Trust, 70, 121, 125, 129
Twelve Steps of AA, 103–109,
  142

Valium, 43, 51
Values (moral/spiritual), 19,
  22, 25

Washburn, Scott, 152
Waverer, 95

Wegscheider-Cruse, Sharon,
  129
Wilson, Bill, 102
Withdrawal, 66
Woititz, Janet, 92

Yancey, Philip, 123
York, David and Phyllis,
  89, 90

Stephen J. Van Cleave, M.D.

Stephen Van Cleave has been involved in the treatment of substance abuse since 1970. He serves as the medical director of T.O.U.C.H. (Transforming Others Under Christ's Hand) drug rehabilitation program. Dr. Van Cleave is the founder and medical director of Community Health Resources, which is an outpatient substance-abuse treatment program in the San Antonio, Texas area. He also serves as associate medical director of Health By Design, which provides fitness and medical evaluations for executives of major corporations. Dr. Van Cleave graduated from the University of Houston and the University of Texas Medical School in San Antonio. He is board certified in both the specialties of internal medicine and emergency medicine. He has provided consultation in the drug-abuse field for several major U. S. corporations, and has testified on adolescent drug abuse before the U. S. Senate Subcommittee on Children, Youth and Families. He has appeared on Dr. James Dobson's "Focus on the Family" radio program discussing families and drug abuse. He and his wife Carol have three daughters: Heather, Kimberly, and Stephanie.

Walter Byrd, M.D.

Walter Byrd is medical director of the Substance Abuse Program at Memorial Hospital of Garland, in Texas, and staff psychiatrist at the Minirth-Meier Clinic in Dallas. Formerly he was director of psychiatric services at Liberty University in Lynchburg, Virginia, and chairman of the department of psychiatry of Virginia Baptist Hospital in Lynchburg. Dr. Byrd is a graduate of the University of Mississippi and the University of Texas Medical School. He and his wife Karen have four children.

Kathy Revell, R.N., C.A.D.A.C.

Kathleen Revell is a certified alcohol and drug abuse counselor, and is the director of the Substance Abuse Program at Memorial Hospital of Garland, in Texas. She received her nurses' training at The Independence Sanitarium and Hospital, Independence, Missouri, and graduated from Graceland College, Lamoni, Iowa. She has over thirteen years of clinical experience in the substance-abuse treatment field, and has served as vice-president of the Texas state chapter of the National Nurses Society on Addictions. Kathy and her husband Roger reside in Garland. They are the parents of two children, Andy and Amy.